Captivators for Christ

Captivators for Christ

R. C. Milco

WESTBOW
PRESS®
A DIVISION OF THOMAS NELSON
& ZONDERVAN

Copyright © 2019 R. C. Milco.

All rights reserved. No part of this book may be used or reproduced by any means, graphic, electronic, or mechanical, including photocopying, recording, taping or by any information storage retrieval system without the written permission of the author except in the case of brief quotations embodied in critical articles and reviews.

Unless otherwise noted, scripture quotations are taken from the NEW AMERICAN STANDARD BIBLE®, Copyright © 1960, 1962, 1963, 1968, 1971, 1972, 1973, 1975, 1977, 1995 by The Lockman Foundation. Used by permission.

Scripture quotations marked NIV are taken from THE HOLY BIBLE, NEW INTERNATIONAL VERSION®, NIV® Copyright © 1973, 1978, 1984, 2011 by Biblica, Inc.® Used by permission. All rights reserved worldwide WestBow Press books may be ordered through booksellers or by contacting:

WestBow Press
A Division of Thomas Nelson & Zondervan
1663 Liberty Drive
Bloomington, IN 47403
www.westbowpress.com
1 (866) 928-1240

Because of the dynamic nature of the Internet, any web addresses or links contained in this book may have changed since publication and may no longer be valid. The views expressed in this work are solely those of the author and do not necessarily reflect the views of the publisher, and the publisher hereby disclaims any responsibility for them.

Any people depicted in stock imagery provided by Getty Images are models, and such images are being used for illustrative purposes only. Certain stock imagery © Getty Images.

ISBN: 978-1-9736-5633-3 (sc)
ISBN: 978-1-9736-5635-7 (hc)
ISBN: 978-1-9736-5634-0 (e)

Library of Congress Control Number: 2019903178

Print information available on the last page.

WestBow Press rev. date: 03/28/2019

With gratitude to Julie, who, as a sister in Christ, lovingly exhorted me to not squander a stewardship.

For those who are still "enemies of the cross of Christ" (Philippians 3:18).

Contents

Preface xi

Entrusting

Starving for Truth 3
On Display 7
No Dependence 10
Divorced! 14
Reframing 18

Leaving Space

"Notice of Change of Terms and Right to Opt Out" 25
Ingredients for an Upset Stomach 28
A Mournful Giver? 32
Entrapment No. 279 35
Candor on a Sensitive Subject 39
Upfront 45
"Content" with Sin 49
Bloodstained Upholstery 52
Compassionate Rebuke 57
Friendly Fire 61
Our Lot in Life 65

Crying Out

Singing in the Dark 73
The Action Prevented 77
Successfully Submitted 80
Placid Tumult 84
Anti-Septic 87
"Let Them Ask Me" 90
Peering Past 94

Remembering Christ

"Forgettery" 99
Reproached, Yet Welcoming 103
In the Margins 107
No Returns 110
"I Will Repay It" 114
"Do Not Be Grieved" 118
Incapacitated 122
The Litmus Test 125
Our Boast 130

Showing Mercy

"Not Overwhelmed" 135
An Invitation 141
Sweetness 145
Midair 150
Dedicated to M. E. 156
An Empty-Handed Guest 160
"Let Me Hate" 164

Afterword 169
Reconciled! 171
Endnotes 175

So, as those who have been chosen of God, holy and beloved, put on a heart of compassion, kindness, humility, gentleness and patience; bearing with one another, and forgiving each other, whoever has a complaint against anyone; just as the Lord forgave you, so also should you.

—Colossians 3:12–13

Preface

Forgiveness is the lynchpin of any relationship we could enjoy with God Himself (Rom. 5:1). It is the work Satan most wills to undermine (2 Cor. 2:10–11), and it is our most prized gifting as we walk on this globe (1 Pet. 2:2).

We are sorely mistaken to believe that our lives must be void of the pangs of injustice, that we are simply here to be "recipients only" of God's free and merciful pardon but never to be imposed upon to bear the *other* side of forgiveness. We exist for something far more purposeful and insanely more intentional than to be the mere "end goal" of God's rich mercies (Titus 3:5). Any wounds we experience this side of heaven are beautiful entry points for the Gospel's declaration.

In Christ's death, we behold "the justice of God satisfied and the love of God demonstrated."[1] Let us be swift to recall that "unless He moves on our behalf, we are damned"[2]— and from that sobering recognition, to then declare with utmost conviction that, just as Christ no longer condemns our fellow man (John 3:17), neither do we (see John 8:11).

The pages in this book are designed to answer a question that arose during a Bible study discussion on Romans 12: How are we to bless those who persecute us? The reality is that we are simply given "distribution privileges," much as the disciples who enjoyed sharing the loaves and fish the Lord had multiplied (Matt. 14:19); nothing originates within ourselves.

Yet, as we remove the offense from the offender by releasing him from the onus of punishment,[3] we will perennially find ourselves faced with the question: "Can any lose, labour, or suffer too much for Him, who gave His beloved Son to be the Sacrifice for their sins, that they might be made the righteousness of God in Him?"[4]

As we experience both the potency of His forgiveness, and His pleasure to extend the same to others *through* us, may God "fulfill every desire for goodness and the work of faith with power, so that the name of our Lord Jesus will be glorified in us, and we in Him, according to the grace of our God and the Lord Jesus Christ" (2 Thess. 1:11–12).

Entrusting

Therefore, those also who suffer according to the will of God shall entrust their souls to a faithful Creator in doing what is right.

—1 Peter 4:19

Starving for Truth[5]

The most distressing place to stand? Undoubtedly the scale at the doctor's office would rank topmost. While I no longer experience quite the "funhouse" effect of staring at the mirror with my physical eyes while mentally reading a completely warped image, residue occasionally surfaces. And that brings with it remembrances of a season in which I, definitively unregenerate, was masking my prideful endeavors to atone for my own iniquity.

Triggered by a friend's talk of engagement just on the precipice of our entering college, the descent into food restriction came amidst the sudden shock that, at age seventeen, I could reside in a state so hideously unprepared for marriage. I was longing desperately for the kind of vulnerable, transparent union of which my friend spoke, yet recoiling equally at the thought of being discovered as an unworthy mess of a sinner. I had heard grace preached. Every Saturday before the message was delivered from the pulpit, I overheard the preview of my father's sermon as he finalized the wording. Yet the veracity of Christ's merit rang hollow in my disbelieving soul.

Proudly convinced of my exceptionality, I surmised that the scope of my sinfulness exceeded God's capacity to pardon so I would take matters into my own hands. The days I spent reveling in the laborious toil of self-punishment persisted as I took twisted delight in hearing my stomach roil over the mere scent of a facial soap; as I playfully observed my wristwatch, on its tightest setting, nearly slide down to my elbow; and as I mentally noted the number of ribs I could count while looking in the mirror. The deprivation was accomplishing both the chastisement I believed necessary and the unexpected bonus of an amazing rush of control.

After my first semester of college wore down, and my body along with it, my parents took the initiative to opt me out of the college scene for a medical leave. My stubbornness then bore out in full tenacity, complete with a host of deceptions that aimed to veil my true motives, my actual eating habits, and the inner turmoil. What disillusionment to realize that "an apple a day" did very little to keep the doctor away. Instead, the old saying incited a flurry of visits. The doctor's scale, as well as the scale at home, became to me an indicator of my worth. Actually, it was a measure in my own eyes of how close I was to rendering myself loveable. Every direction toward loss I counted as a small goal *gained*, although I began to perceive how the next five pounds was never enough. By the time medical tests revealed that my body had gone the more extreme route of metabolizing my brain for survival, I landed on a hospital bed, awash in shame.

As I sat in a loathsome hospital gown alongside my mother, crumpled by the weight of my vigorous efforts blown up in my face, the words that came forth were of sheer confession and horrid unbelief. With my wrists held forth and my spirit provoked within me, I cried out, "The nails should have gone through *these!*"

Without denying the truth of my grieved appraisal, she

avowed to the reality of Christ's unconditional love as a Rescuer. "He would have come, were you the only person on this earth." Suddenly, I was shattered by the weight of His mercy, freely given. How could this God, who knew my every sin, offer with such personal and tender deliverance (Rom. 2:4) a sacrifice so defiant of any repayment (Rom. 11:34–35)? His truth nourished my lie-ravaged soul.

As one gospel primer[6] words it with succinct tones of awe,

> God ... allowed His future and present wrath against me to be completely propitiated by Jesus, who bore it upon Himself while on the cross. Consequently, God now has only love, compassion, and deepest affection for me, and this love is without any admixture of wrath whatsoever.
>
> I don't deserve any of this, even on my best day; but this is my salvation.

The year following was fraught with battling the "old" will. Each thought, "taken captive to the obedience of Christ" (2 Cor. 10:5), had to be recalibrated with Scripture's pronouncements. Every decision to avoid the unhealthy patterns, ever as I recovered physiologically from the nutrient depletion, was an hour-by-hour engagement.

Even two decades later, the residual effects remain, sometimes with a subtle reintroduction of a warped report from the mirror that prods me to detect my rising doubts over the longevity and authenticity of God's inundating, enduring pardon. There are days as well, when I anticipate stepping onto the doctor's scale, in which mild trepidation arises, not because I fear there will be a resurgence of that former "death wish" (thankfully, God wrought the demise of that volition) but because the undercurrent of deception still finds room to occasionally taunt the truth my regenerate being is slow to grasp.

Yet in spite of any physical place where my feet may stand, the *Source* of my acceptance is firm and unrelenting (Rom. 15:7; *cf* Ps. 49:15; 2 Cor. 6:17–18). Christ's offering of Himself is the replete atonement that cleanses our conscience from dead works (Heb. 9:14). In His infinitely compassionate reclamation, our Lord has dealt with utter mercy toward the very ones who had trampled His priceless worth.

> It was for freedom that Christ set us free; therefore keep standing firm and do not be subject again to a yoke of slavery.
>
> —Galatians 5:1

On Display

Unsolicited trials shouldn't constitute "opportunities." Yet how I was checked in my wrong thinking when a fellow church member wrote,

> As with all things, God will ultimately hold me accountable with how I managed this disease and used conversations about my cancer to point others toward Christ.[7]

The fact that he viewed his illness as a stewardship revamped everything. How many a hardship has appeared as an accidental handiwork that could not, upon arrival at the doorstep, produce its misplaced invitation? It is worthy of being erased but not entertained, for surely it would only hamper all the work of getting on with life! "Abounding with opportunity" scarcely registers in my mindset.

Wastefulness careens through the misunderstandings we bear. If aches and afflictions are passageways, not dead ends, then at our full disposal are veritable seedbeds for variegated testimonies of Christ to espouse His fidelity toward the faithless, His fulfillment of our legal debt, and His declaring the vile spotless.

Divinely bestowed hazards become not roadblocks but

throughways apportioned before time for us to step into with grace (Eph. 2:10). Determined as completely His, we serve as vessels ravaged by the battery of trials—internal and external but not eternal! And we are limited in our telling of Him to unbelievers by the paltry substance of time. In the ages to come, we will be displayed as the incontrovertible evidence depicting the "surpassing riches of His grace" (Eph. 2:7), but in the interim, the world is supplied His own personal testimony through us (Matt. 10:18). We are fitted as ambassadors through whom He makes an appeal for all rebels to be reconciled to God through Christ (2 Cor. 5:18–20).

On the macro scale, every believer's privilege is identical. Each is made a conduit: a recipient of God's ministry—to echo the same. Before the penetrating eyes of those who know us to be the anomaly (Phil. 2:14–15), God has sanctioned us to chase down the hiding, as He did (Gen. 3:8–9) to announce the peace treaty (Isa. 52:7) written with His own Son's blood.[8]

Our stewardship, also referred to as suffering, enables hands that would otherwise be clenched to honor Him who was our purchase price. Through a Mediator who stood outside our hopeless condition (1 Tim. 2:5–6), we who had not received mercy now have (1 Pet. 2:10). Our proper receiving of that independently rendered gift flows from our ensuring that others likewise taste its relief (see 2 Cor. 4:1–6).

We bear witness *of* Him who has lovingly made us objects of His compassion (Eph. 5:2; Rev. 1:5), but we also stand as His masterfully appointed "lumps" of glory (see Rom. 9:21, 23) to bear witness *for* Him. We are *evidence but also entreaty, proof but also petition.*

Heralds now of His ability to refashion "crooked hearts twisted up,"[9] we become His injunction to perishing ones to believe in Him (Acts 16:31). We are commissioned to reach fellow creatures as incompetent as we were in recognizing (Eph. 2:1) or remedying (Rom. 5:6, 8) our naturally "wretched, miserable, poor, blind, and naked" beings (Rev. 3:17). Just as He bade us come, He bids men still.

Ours is His mighty entrusting, the downward-plunged gifting of "standing witness" of the Prince of life (Acts 3:15) — the Righteousness we disowned and whom God permitted to be slain so that murderers might be spared (v. 14; *cf* Isa. 53:3, 8, 11–12; Acts 2:23). Troubling and burdensome though it first appears, the plague that lends us voice could not be eclipsed in either the heftiness or holiness of the guardianship charged to us. We, partakers of the divine nature (2 Pet. 1:4), are empowered to pierce the darkness with the proclamation that the King of Glory rent the heavens and came down (Isa. 64:1; John 1:9–11, 14) to avail Himself to helpless creatures, simply because it was "according to all the desire of His soul to do so" (see 1 Sam. 23:20).

Let us not be careless with the commission He has lent us. It constitutes His chosen instrument of eternal consequence.

No Dependence

When taken in light of its recipients, God's giving is preposterous. The supremely good Giver, from whom "every good and perfect gift" originates (James 1:17 NIV), has inflicted upon Himself heartache for those who had taken up arms against Him by provoking (Jer. 25:7) and wearying (Isa. 1:14) Him with iniquities. He has "remembered His covenant" with those who "despised the oath" (Ezek. 16:59–60), forsook Him (v. 32), and took Him as a fool. He has presented His heart to creatures who neither esteemed His self-disclosure or selflessness. He surrendered Himself—yet we scorned Him, rudely castigating His heartfelt, magnanimous offer with a pernicious fascination over the gods of our own making.

This God whom we serve is independent of anything we are or could return to Him. Indeed, He "lends, expecting nothing in return" (Luke 6:35). Were we a faithful lot, were we pure in deed, were our spirits turned to Him as His is toward our own (see Hos. 11:8), then the volatile distinction may not transpire with such maddening haste.

God has not given to the worthy. Boundless in His delight to supply us that which is of greatest worth, He pours forth from His hands till nothing remains (Rom. 8:32). It is as if a distinguished forfeiture pronounces the most clearly that He would part with all He holds dear so we might understand the intense authenticity of His love—even when unreciprocated.

Still, we would be mistaken to imagine that such unprejudiced, undemanding love equates to an obsequence that bears out as a doormat. He invites not abuse but the unmitigated awe over His relating to us "not on the basis of deeds which we have done" (Titus 3:5) but on the thoughts He thinks toward us (Ps. 40:5). His divine empathy, originating within Him, proactively treats us as beneficiaries regardless of our past. "So then it does not depend on the man who wills or the man who runs, but on God who has mercy" (Rom. 9:16).

For anyone who has had to operate in that alien paradigm—where the mettle of the recipient is not the basis of the interaction—adopting His "independence" might not seem feasible. Our propensity to "do good" is generally reserved only for those who have first shown us favor: to love and lend to the people whom we think will surely (perhaps even more completely) repay us for the kindness (Luke 6:32–34).

To embrace the pattern He established amounts to the "wrecking-ball" experience of having our every unsteady mooring clearly exposed and displaced. For we cannot any longer veil our generous acts with the pretenses of returning the warmth proffered us. Unfastened by the levity of the task, we discover in ourselves that presumptions of entitlement wage a hefty war. Whether we would dare voice the expectation, we long for the treatment that sets us in dignified display before onlooking eyes. Our fledgling sense of "security," rooted in every errant direction, delights in the bolstering afforded by the tender and tenacious care of those around us.

We are also laid bare as those who avoid penalties. When handed the choice between showering our energies and investments on those who could make some return and those who had no means, we would rarely think like our Father in seeking out the very ones who could never show us like reception (see Luke 14:12–13).

And, perhaps at the core of our struggle, the crumbling foundation surfaces when He instructs us that proactively loving those who curse us will compose the wealth of our labor. To desist from vengeance may be acceptable in our sight, but to exert powerful effort in feeding and comforting (Rom. 12:20) him who has actively made our lives miserable seems unreasonable, unjustifiable—and unmerciful to the one being given the command.

Yet what we miss—in our badgering the Lord's patience with our defiance—is that He ties blessings with each of these gracious acts. If we could view it aright, the artifice of the endeavor is grueling to our flesh; but the profit is to both the offender and ourselves! By the carrying out of such hard decrees, God has interwoven our obedience to Him with the furtherance of what He can achieve in our character and composition, as well as with what He can credit to those whom He saved "for good deeds" (see Titus 2:14; 3:8).

For, in "not demanding back" what has been taken from our possession (Luke 6:30), we are transformed into those who are named "sons of the Most High," who is Himself "kind to ungrateful and evil men" (v. 35). Our resemblance to our Father is solidified. And by inviting "the poor, crippled, lame, and blind" (Luke 14:13) to share in what is ours, we will find repayment in the One who has every means at

His disposal (Lk. 14:14; cf Ps. 50:10–12). And, in placing ourselves in the path of the ones who have harmed us, seeking intentional ways to "overcome evil with good" (Rom. 12:21), we are assured that—by deferring to the Lord to mete out any needed justice (v. 19)—our beings are freed to "respect what is right in the sight of all men" (v. 17) and to "be at peace" so far as we are able (v. 18). Subjecting our inaccurate appraisals to His flawless one will ensure for us the liberty to engage on a level of God-fearing "patience, kindness, goodness, and self-control" (Gal. 5:22–23) that will cause us to function as "blameless and innocent, children of God above reproach" (Phil. 2:15).

The God in whom our salvation originates (Jon. 2:9) has chiseled out for us the role of autonomous giving. While the exercise clashes against everything our natural bent would select, still it is the pursuit that carefully calibrates us with our original design. As Image-reflectors of the Master—who "does according to His will in the host of heaven and among the inhabitants of earth" (Dan. 4:35)—we discover that the Deviser of our wellbeing, who extricated us from our shame, furnishes us the role that most dignifies both benefactor and recipient. For, in His determination to prosper us with such fierceness, we have the latitude to imitate His likeness toward others—and, in participating in His handiwork, we preach to ourselves and others that, just as we held no sway in the *endowment* of His compassion, neither could we bring about its *erasure*.

Divorced!

Contrition throbs with rawness over what cannot be undone. Powerless to rectify the past, the surging mental turmoil may leave us bludgeoned:

> I am tormented by the thought … that I didn't do as you asked me as a matter of course. To be frank, I can't think what made me behave as I did. … it preys on my mind … because it's the kind of thing one can never make up for. So all I can do is to ask you to forgive my weakness then. I know now for certain that I ought to have behaved differently.[10]

One particular time haunts me like none other. Out of fearfulness of man's opinion of me, out of a hope that I could prop up a needless reputation, out of a very evident lack of concern for what my actions would do to those I loved, I took leave of a precious community without giving so much as any disclosure that I was even contemplating departure. The havoc unleashed on those who picked up all my pieces was unfair: a wretched closure toward those who, in utter selflessness and support, had always looked out for my best interests; who had, in truth, with Christ-reliance, saturated this life with grace incarnate.

I wince—not because the Lord's hand has not relieved me from the weight of wrongdoing by cleansing me in the aftermath of confession (1 John 1:9) but because the dissembling still needs purging. It is not that I would deny my *accountability* in past actions (or the vile heart motives swirling around such) but that I would eagerly deny any *association* with that "old" nature (Eph. 4:22) that propagated that hardship toward those very dear to me.

For those of us who have been on the receiving end of forgiveness—foremost through Christ's compassionate pardon, and then through the mercy of a fellow human being who had every reason to expel us from relationship—there is a bleeding triumph. When our aggrieved spirits burst forth with the steely consciousness of our responsibility for irreversible damages incurred, there is soul-splitting relief to be dealt with apart from our natural constitution (Ps. 103:10–12).

None but a heart laden with compunction can appreciate the detection quite as somberly—not simply that we are diseased beyond our comprehension (Jer. 17:9) but that the Holy Spirit laboriously incites our *hatred* for iniquity as He "convicts us concerning sin and righteousness and judgment" (see John 16:8–11). We practice harmonizing *why we sin*, as born sinners (Ps. 51:5) with *why He came*—in order to save His people from their sinful selves (Matt. 1:21). We unearth the daunting spiritual law that "sin will kill us forever, if we are not spared by the Lord's dying."

From that place of "breakage," with our mouths in the dust (Lam. 3:29), proprietary rights crystallize: "We have sinned, do to us whatever seems good to You … " (Judges

10:15). The depravity that lurks within elicits steep veneration for the expensive Blood wielding deliverance.

A turnaround of soul arises. For in our revulsion over how we have, in a spiritual adultery, defied and wounded (Ezek. 6:9) the Maker of heaven and earth, we come to discern how "nothing can be cheap to us which is costly to God."[11] Lament pours forth in response to our uncleansed hands, our impure hearts, and our double-mindedness (James 4:8–9) as, reeling, we discover afresh that we bear a unified heart with those condemning the Righteous One (Matt. 27:22–23, 25). "Repentance without regret" is His ambition in us (see 2 Cor. 7:10), and a contrite heart and lowly spirit are eye-catching to our humble Sovereign (see Ps. 34:18; Isa. 57:15; 66:2).

Even on days accompanied by sharp remembrances that sin blatantly defaults on its every promise, He continues faithfully "working in us that which is pleasing in His sight" (Heb. 13:21). Entailed in all the stripping away of everything grotesque will be the added grace: that He, who fortifies our spirits to zealously rectify any wrongs we have committed (2 Cor. 7:11), deals with us as those who have been entirely divorced from the old man we were. Since our full culpability was dealt with in Christ's body and ministry (in His accepting the punishment and accomplishing the purity that should have been ours), we are fully divested—"robbed" as it were—of the malignant nature once composing "us."

As the beloved hymn proclaiming His triumph cries out,

> My sin—oh, the bliss of this glorious thought!—
> My sin, not in part but the whole,
> Is nailed to the cross, and I bear it no more,
> Praise the Lord, praise the Lord, O my soul![12]

We are the "already but not yet resurrected fallen men"[13] who stand groomed for a presentation before the Father's throne. The concluding remarks at that judgment bench will be that we are found "holy and blameless and beyond reproach" (Col. 1:22). "Great joy" will unfold in the presence (Jude 1:24) of Him who made us "alive together with Him, having forgiven us all our transgressions, having canceled out the certificate of debt consisting of decrees against us" (Col. 2:13–14).

We are not who we *were* (see 1 Cor. 6:9–11), but neither are we those whom we *will* be. Take heart; He will not be deterred (Phil. 1:6).

Reframing

I had put myself to bed at an unusually early hour, with the light from across the hallway creeping in through the slits around the doorframe. Somehow this hour had not reached me in the direct aftermath of discovering the betrayal, but more than a year after it had been confirmed, and my mind had expended itself wearily integrating the peculiar paradigm into my daily existence. It wasn't in the shockwaves that the reverberations were felt but suddenly, in the debilitating realization that, even were I to taste the peaceful escape of death, I could not evade the consciousness of what had irrevocably transpired. Thankfully, when exiting this life would have most appealed, the tainted recognition of what it could not overcome at least allowed me to relinquish its consideration.

Days crashed in with looming exhaustion, the emotional toil of survival being paramount. Hourly decisions of the will to exercise forgiveness, to receive to my core the wrongness of another's choices (whether compelled or undertaken with scorn of soul, I knew not, but gargantuan in their repercussions upon my spirit, I well understood) inundated me at each turn. The tangible reminders—typical triggers when someone loses a loved one but not hugely muted in a breach of trust—came at their unexpected moments, propelling me into the calculated mental assent that choosing to spare the offender any malice was my only basis for operation.

The visceral reactions bored their way into my deepest recesses, as I wrangled with sentiments I had never before entertained. With increasing rawness to each abrasion, I slid into a stoical stance, cognizant that I was ceasing to feel yet glad of it. At least I could cope. At least the breathing was a little less jagged. Entering the eye of the storm, where all was quieter, carved out the thinking space that swirling emotions otherwise ambushed.

And yet, where does that leave a person who must absorb the fitful throbbing of a contorted life, which seems trampled by another's sinning and never to unburden itself from the full magnitude? Where does one start picking up one foot after another to begin that road back to hope, not in circumstances (as those have well proven unstable and illusory) but in the sense of not relying too much on sinful man, or on self-impressed expectations of a life "on course"—since those faulty indices have already pronounced their fruitlessness?

There were hours when, through poetry or journaling, I could bleed out the confounding predicament of confusion and angst, but on the whole, I was too shortsighted, too self-engrossed (as pain is wont to foment) to recognize the payment by which I was secured. Or rather, enmeshed in disillusionment, I played with the razor-edged shards of my dreams, shattered, and lost the grander sweep of what the Lord was unrelentingly accomplishing.

He had bought me (1 Cor. 6:19–20). Neither the purchase price (1 Pet. 1:18–19) nor His prerogative to wield me for His pleasure (2 Tim. 2:20–21; Rev. 4:11) were up for debate. I had lost any intelligent understanding that I now served a new Master, no longer held in bondage to my former slave master of lust and hedonism but under the captivating purview of Righteousness Himself (Rom. 6:18; *cf* Jer. 23:6). I erred in surmising that the current, temporary circumstances were all He would tell of this life, that He had sorely undervalued what I counted of greatest worth and had pushed to the side my every concern, even those I had most tenderly petitioned Him for, when my heart was most vulnerable in the offering.

He has afforded me perspective enough since that hour to comprehend that not only is treachery not the lasting word (how insufficient it is to compete with His holy endeavors!) but that it was on account of my grief-saturated, though faulty, perception that I thrust myself into heartache from which I could have steered clear. Had I, in those most noteworthy pangs of wondering about His nature, grounded myself (shored up my mind and truthfully taken hold with a willful conviction) that He was adamantly defending my very desires (those that were based on godly determination to see His will carried out in this life), then I might have appreciated the fuller scope—that He was actively listening to the cry of the one who feared Him (Ps. 145:19), that He was withholding nothing good from the one who was walking uprightly (Ps. 84:11), that His wonders were many, and that His plans on my behalf could not even be recounted, too numerous were they (Ps. 40:5), that—even in that cringing moment, when my palate was sated on tears more than any morsel of food (Ps. 42:3)—He was actively fulfilling the very desire He had planted within me (Ps. 37:4), that there would be life out of death and hope out of despair.

It is one thing to give vent to a woeful spirit, but it is far different to exhaust our misery in the confidence of the One who compassionately hears and proactively cares. Being wholly aligned with our Master's will may relieve nothing of our trial but will serve in perfecting the relationship until we are firmly grounded in His being *for* us (Ps. 118:6). And from that point, we are reframed to cry out, in even the darkness impeding our vision, "All my springs of joy are in You" (Ps. 87:7).

Leaving Space

"You shall not take vengeance, nor bear any grudge ... but you shall love your neighbor as yourself; I am the LORD."

—Leviticus 19:18

"Notice of Change of Terms and Right to Opt Out"

The Almighty, who accomplishes all that "His soul desires" (Job 23:13; Ps. 115:3; 135:6), can never be thwarted in His methods (Job 42:2; Isa. 14:27; 43:13; Dan. 4:35). While I cannot pretend He would alter midstream the requirements of obedience, the finite mind perceives His plan's unfolding as a graduated revelation of expenditures.

Yet our remaining time—post-"flesh walking" (Rom. 8:4; Eph. 4:22)—exists to be expended for the will of God (see 1 Pet. 4:1–2) Hardships are inherent. The Apostle Paul is unapologetic about kingdom entry only coming through many tribulations (Acts 14:22).

Still, residing within my calloused chest, miscreant allegations prop themselves up against the One I suppose has changed the rules. Spelunking the caverns of commitment suddenly entails depths exceeding my original calculations (e.g., a "notice of change of terms") and brusquely triggers my agitation that I received no accompanying "right-to-opt-out" form.

Much as I argue that my declination would be conducted *honorably*, I am harassed by the non-existent escape route. For the sake of self-protection, for the seduction of comfort's lure, I repeatedly recalculate an "easier path," blinded to how I am falling prey to the Enemy's tactical tool of concession.

The "finish line" is nowhere in sight; the strategic plan to simply pay a "restocking fee" for damaged goods refuses to materialize. Prayers aim low. I would rather rack up penalties by terminating the transaction than be enjoined to the stretching of abiding in the unresolved.

But such truths only belie a contractual heart that rarely peers beyond any immediate discomfiture to behold, with awe and radical gratitude, that my senses are barely perceiving more than the fringes of His activity (Job 26:14). Covenant-establishing and Covenant–honoring, this Lord defines fidelity with His sweeping commitment (Heb. 6:17–18). His heart longs to interpose with a fuller benefit than any our imaginations could pave the way to anticipate (Isa. 64:3–4; 1 Cor. 2:9), and He will not be deprived of the pleasure of bestowing on His creatures every good thing He has apportioned to them (Ps. 34:10; 84:11).

God is "never grieved to give us good," which ought rightly to assure me that He who has measured out the lines for my inheritance (Ps. 16:5–6; 47:4) will continually afford me every (lesser) earthly measurement according to His suitable delineation. Were there any less taxing alternative as effective, He—who "does not afflict willingly or grieve the sons of men" (Lam. 3:33)—would have undoubtedly supplied such means. Unsolved tensions can still lean into His benevolent care (Ps. 103:13).

For truthfully, Jesus refused to renege on His love-drenched undertaking on our behalf, when He was fully cognizant of every shred of humiliation that awaited Him. His deliberate approach and descent into our humanity were arrangements about which He was thoroughly apprised, and which He accepted. He was unchanged in His volition (Ps. 15:4).

While the profound ignominy of our obligations may disturb our unsuspecting gaze, can we detect the contradiction of design were we to purge ourselves of prior pledges? Can we rightly surmise that, if His beloved children are incited to imitate God (Eph. 5:1), it is outright defecting to exhibit anything shy of His well-spent love (v. 2)?

Ingredients for an Upset Stomach

Un-forgiveness takes many forms.

Somewhere between failed attempts to learn my family's heritage language and high school research that dogged me with shadows of my ancestors' backstory of flight from persecution, I acquired a haughty distaste for the country that, to present day, absolves itself of responsibility for its crimes against humanity. The onus to "never forget" clings closely.

More current genocides, perpetrated by the same religious group, have taken shape before my eyes through online news reports. The dismantling of whole towns and villages, the widespread onslaught and abuses, the callous murder and the victorious cries over crushing the despised people group—all reverberate with the Satanic pleasure of erasing the life of any Image-bearer. The devil, a murderer from the beginning (John 8:44), brandishes whichever willing instruments arise in each generation to continue his mission of destroying the divine dignity bequeathed to mankind.

And then not long ago, a fellow tenant, who knew my lineage and had himself emigrated from a refugee camp to the United States as he evaded the genocide within his own borders, requested that I proof his grad school thesis. The content was not some impersonal conglomeration of research and statistics but a decided passion over lives touched and broken by active hatred that reveled to display its full, egregious expressions. May it ever be abhorrent to discover that—whether the targeted groups of families were driven from their villages by starvation marches, or taken by train to remote locales (to the same end), or hanged, or "dumped alive into remote masses of water"[14]—such souls were despised simply for their being of the country's minority faith, or of a bloodline somehow deemed inferior by the ruling party.

For as much as I would have expected enough distance to have transpired, would have thought myself sufficiently removed from the horrors of days that left my family tree untraceable prior to 1915, two unexpected elements surfaced. For one, there was the sense of *victimization:* I retain little but fragmented stories of how relatives can only remember "running," leaving behind all worldly possessions as they hastily sought the safety their homeland could no longer secure. For another, there was an *arrogant disdain:* the ruling powers responsible, persistently denying culpability, have gone so far as to white out the entire epoch through government-sanctioned "history" books. Both by bearing an injustice needing to be redressed and guarding the entitled "right" to hold the offender in contempt, I was feeding an unforgiving spirit.

And yet, beyond those two ingredients, there is a harder-to-swallow truth. For when I ensconce myself with the notion that I am the trampled one, I operate on the unfounded self-perception of blamelessness. If I glance even briefly, I will grasp how my hands were bloodied, along with every other breath-given human, for the persecuted death march of God's Beloved Son (Matt. 27:31–33).

While He was by no means victimized—He was a ready offering to be arrested (John 18:4) and struck (Isa. 50:6)—the travesty against Him was the greatest committed. This Man, God incarnate, voluntary Rescuer, stood accursed: a criminal's condemnation laid upon the Perfect Son of God while the guilty lawbreaker was set free in His place, "the just for the unjust" (1 Pet. 3:18).

We are not the wronged party. Yes, men inflict heartless deeds upon each other—all of which find their just satisfaction in either the offender's eternal payment or in the offender's eternal Substitute, Christ Jesus, our Lord—but how can we gaze at His bludgeoned brow and scarred side—at His languishing in agony over the spiritual separation He experienced from His Precious Father—and dare presume we have "rights" still to defend? There was no sin in Him (1 Pet. 2:22). He was undeserving to the utmost, and yet—for the sake of lives entirely dependent upon His singular intervention—He embraced the full penalty of our every vile deed and wicked thought.

Recently I was reminded that justice is double-edged, with punishment for the oppressor and rescue for the oppressed.[15] In the case of Calvary, the complete reverse played out—albeit, according to divine planning (Acts 2:23). Proverbs 17:15 speaks to the outrageous exchange when it recounts, "He who justifies the wicked and he who condemns the righteous, both of them alike are an abomination to the LORD." To set free the one who should be penalized is a complete miscarriage of justice, as is holding to account the one who should be cleared. Yet God alone—powerful enough to accomplish the plan and willful enough to pursue it—firmly resolved Himself to His Son's subjection under the load of our debts. Romans 3:26 asserts that Jesus' death comprises the full array of evidence that God is *just,* by leveling the proper verdict against transgressions, and that He is also the *justifier,* by vindicating through faith each one who trusts in His timeless atonement, which resounds through the ages as "finished" work.

Were our vision corrected, we would begin to trace that no one is beholden to us, that our autobiography is less "victim" and far more "villain." If the solitary attainment for our pardon necessitated "those cruel nails, open wounds, and God Himself gasping for air … And … the infinite, blistering volcano of God's righteous anger meant for us"[16] falling upon His Beloved, may our pride be ever ruined to trace how we must be "more wicked than we could ever completely grasp."[17]

Exclusively Christ's indebted ones, we are those whose sins He bore in His own body on the cross (1 Pet. 2:24). Any claims of abuse or calls for vengeance suffer inevitable collapse when a bloodstained torture device, groaning beneath the hefty love of the Master of the universe, bespeaks the *true* violation.

A Mournful Giver?

My mom exemplifies a cheerful giver. Stockpiling toiletries for shoebox collections and closing out annuities constitute two beloved hobbies of a woman who delights in sounding forth the Gospel through the charities she supports. The Christ-like generosity, only enlarged throughout her spiritual journey, causes both marveling and chagrin within this heart; for, much as I would love to emulate such benevolence, the ruefully calculated opening of my hand only proves the stinginess soundly throbbing through these veins.

If, as a friend once described certain portions of Scripture, our souls find particular passages as abrasive as a cheese grater,[18] Deuteronomy 15 especially scrapes me. In verses directed to the sons of Israel, Moses depicts the hallmark graciousness of the Lord's people, themselves ongoing recipients. Instruction includes "not hardening one's heart, or closing one's hand from one's poor brother, but freely opening one's hand and generously lending him sufficient for his lack" (v. 7–8).

Reiterated three verses later, the idea is then intensified in between: "Beware that there is no base thought in your heart ... and your eye is [not] hostile toward your poor brother ... your heart shall not be grieved when you give ..." (v. 9–10). Both the Lord's deliverance from prior bondage

("You shall remember that you were a slave in the land of Egypt, and the LORD your God redeemed you" [v. 15]) and the promise of divine favor ("The LORD your God will bless you in all your work and in all your undertakings" [v. 10]) fortify the negative commands with incentive enough to propel such ample lending.

While the gear shifting from material to spiritual borrowing may pose a hurdle, each believer has experienced a "year of remission" (v. 8) in which an insurmountable debt to the perfect Law was paid in full (see Rom. 10:4). God lent to us His flawless purity. We are beneficiaries of an exodus from iniquity. Our hands are now equipped to bestow upon others whatever is in our means to grant. Joyously, humbly our good will can be exercised "in proportion to his distress and poverty, and our ability."[19]

In his commentary on the passage, Matthew Henry delineates the principle at work: "Grudge not a kindness to thy brother; and distrust not the providence of God … but, on the contrary, let it be … a satisfaction of soul to thee to think that thou art honouring God with thy substance." He continues, "If we cannot trust the borrower, we must trust God, and lend, hoping for nothing again in this world, but expecting it will be recompensed in the resurrection of the just" (Luke 6:35; 14:14).[20]

In that God-ward trust, the Apostle Paul notes how the Macedonians gave mercifully out of their exceeding poverty (2 Cor. 8:1–5), fully assured that their Provider would endow them with all they required as they extended themselves in generosity. Addressing the evident need presented in the church, this faith-filled people, motivated in response to Christ's eager bestowal of pardon, performed a lavish display of devotion to Him.

When my M.O. has often riveted on the idea of "exchange" (versus letting loose what may never henceforth resurface), the hurdle is elucidated: I maintain a "Belial heart" that conjectures, "I will not lend what I must then be sure to lose."[21] Not only is my nature manifested as diametrically opposed to the Father's (Luke 6:35–36), but my vantage point is challenged as well. There sounds forth a call to forfeiture: to cease cleaving to self-absorbed assertions that highlight "less expensive" methods of giving, to forsake the persistent shortsightedness preoccupied with this life's meager losses, and to renounce the absolute blindness to the One whose open-handedness exempted us from hell through a host of brutal expenditures.

To lament the release of superficial trinkets is to dull our souls to the supreme Sacrifice. Even those deprivations of paramount import in this life will be found shamefully wanting in light of the "out of proportion"[22] glory into which we will step. Rather than endeavoring to ward off adversity and the tabulations of hardship that leave us floundering, true submission before Him cleanses us of misdirected affections and establishes an authentic rehabilitation of attitude. As He subverts our trivial mourning, He teaches us to view aright that, though another's sins may have leveled upon us great fees, the person is not, as we construed, simply "a costly one" but instead "a *priceless* one." And in our remembering, He guides us to no longer sorrow over what leaves our keeping but over whatever leaves us hindered in expressing His likeness *more*.

Entrapment No. 279

Perhaps it is the consequence of growing up in a culture that portrays God as the Welcomer of all *sins*, instead of the mind-blowing Deity-in-the-form-of-Man receiving all sinners to Himself in order to *cure* them (Mk. 2:17), but when I entered a phase of feeling overrun, underpowered, and out of recourse, it helped little to envision a Heavenly Father whose mercies sounded forth with condoning approval for all that was ravaging my spirit. The pools of reasoning, eddying around yet one more entrapment of the devil's contrivance, were restless waters stirring me to fear that fair dealings would never be manifested. Man's gleeful extortion of rights appeared far less debilitating than the extortion of hope that came when God's hand looked too lenient in the face of each wrong.

Yet my arrival into such a predicament issued forth from His desire to teach me more of Himself (Matt. 11:29). If I was beguiled by the contention that only "the sin leading to death" (1 John 5:16) would ever be met with divine censure, then I underestimated the One who—in the direct aftermath of Aaron's eldest sons being consumed for offering an inappropriate sacrifice (Lev. 10:1–2)—declared that "by those who come near Me I will be treated as holy" (v. 3).

With no concern over my being heard, still I walked

away from prayers feeling "restless in my complaint" (Ps. 55:2). Venting and "woe-ing" and aching all felt allowed in the ears of my Father (1 Sam. 1:10, 15–16; Ps. 55:22; 62:8; 1 Pet. 5:7), but rectification felt an expectation I could not reasonably impose on One "too kind," too soft-hearted, to actually bring a man to punishment. I operated under the guise that the only wrath God would ever reveal had already been expended (which, for the sake of salvation, it has; Heb. 9:26), so I could never figure discipline would settle its somber clutches around a transgressing heart that, to my side of living, appeared unstoppable.

My lack of logic was right in keeping with everyone who supposes there are inconsistencies to be found in God's nature, that the "Old Testament God" delivered only vengeance and the "New Testament God" lacked any backbone for meting out retribution. Somehow I missed His compassion toward the Ninevites (Jonah 4:11) and the immediate public deaths of Ananias and Sapphira (Acts 5:5, 10). Forget the idea that Jesus's final showcase of His power is in "judging and waging war in righteousness" (Rev. 19:11)—a sword in His wielding and His robe dipped in blood (v. 13, 15).

It was not that my misunderstanding stemmed from my owning a Bible heretically "slashed" of every plaintive cry of the psalmists (David, most especially), as iterative phrases begged the Lord God of hosts, omnipotent Commander of armies, "Arise, O LORD, confront him, bring him low; deliver my soul from the wicked with Your sword" (Ps. 17:13; 10:12; *cf* 12:5, etc.). It was simply that I had exhausted myself with the wearying misconception that mercy would be God's singular reply to any spirit fraught with iniquity. My analysis required an implosion ...

... which God faithfully delivered. Through serious examination of the prophets, especially Isaiah and Jeremiah, where the cornerstone of God's dealings with His people was loving justice, I came to appreciate His corrective shepherding techniques. Guiding His children back to a path of righteousness—"for His name's sake" (Ps. 23:3)—through measures sometimes so harsh that even His own messengers, serving as intercessory representatives before Him on behalf of His erring nation, would cry out, "in wrath remember mercy" (Hab. 3:2), and "let now Your anger and Your wrath turn away" (Dan. 9:16). As He "naturalized" adopted sons, discipline framed the basic procedure of ensuring holiness (see Heb. 12:8–10).

To one who had many times fathomed myself precluded from His serious consideration—although His scrutinizing eye needed no aid in uncovering all (2 Chron. 16:9; Prov. 15:3; Jer. 23:23–24; cf Zech. 4:10)—my introduction to the times when He drew a firm line beckoned me to pray: "Your God has commanded your strength; show Yourself strong, O God, who have acted on our behalf" (Ps. 68:28).

As the praying drew emboldened hues from the supplications of His own messengers, I found my heart unabashed in laying out arguments (not *against* Him, but *in* Him)—with courage placing itself in the confidence of the One with whom I could "discuss matters of justice" (Jer. 12:1–3). The inconsistencies of flourishing iniquities (Ps. 92:6–7) and "chastened" innocence (Ps. 73:13–14) were nothing unmanageable to the One who meted out to His Anointed Son "the deepest stroke that pierced Him."[23]

On levels I had no power to survey, He knew the largeness of what justice required (see 2 Thess. 1:6–8). If the Resplendent One uniquely surmised the fullness of debt owed Him by "Adam's helpless race"[24] and comprehensively fulfilled payment on man's behalf Himself (Isa. 53:12), then any lesser outstanding fees constituted ramifications fully to be entrusted to His all-wise judicial rendering (2 Thess. 1:5).

Even in the sting of a situation that grace was not about to make "un-done," I lodged myself in the care of the One whose very throne is founded on "righteousness and justice" (Ps. 89:14; 97:2). He is the One in whom no evil dwells (Ps. 5:4; 92:15). Yes, He has availed Himself in the meekness of a Lamb (John 1:29), but He has also interposed in the might of our Advocate, who argued that the guilty ones be credited with His own innocence. We have in Him "a saving defense" (Ps. 28:8) in the one case of import; how much more can we discharge ourselves to His perfect rulings in every other issue of justice in this life (see Luke 18:7–8)?

With zealous compassion He has ruined our strongholds. With ardent love He has toppled our crimes against Him through the proffering of His own life as our ransom. He bids us now to leave space for Him to act in whatever manner is most fitting, to trust Him where our sight can fetch no assurance as pure as His regarding what will most satisfy the need. Falling on His mercy, we have not only the pleasure of ascribing to Him total righteousness (Job 36:3) but also the joy of resounding back to Him the steady assurance that "in You the helpless has hope" (see Job 5:16)!

Candor on a Sensitive Subject

Someone once posed to me the question over how a couple is to heal over past sexual sinning. Christ was gracious in supplying a response, in a message that hopefully pointed both believers toward the saving hope of Calvary.

Thank you for your candor on a highly sensitive subject. Healing from past sins birthed in lust is a matter of delicacy and dependence on the veracity of the cross. Apart from truthfully walking in (abiding in, meditating upon, reveling in, praising Him for) the cleansing He's provided, we always fall prey to the notion that our past defines who are today.

Specifically with sexual sin, Paul writes that immorality is distinct in that every other sin committed is outside the body, but sexual transgressions are against a person's own body (1 Cor. 6:18). The call to "flee quickly" rings throughout the epistles (also 2 Tim. 2:22; *cf* Eph. 5:3) and is accompanied by stern warnings for those who do not seek purity (see 1 Thess. 4:3–6; Heb. 13:4).

As far as what immorality declares against God, Paul writes that it's a rejection of His Spirit, since we are called to sanctification through Him (1 Thess. 4:7–8). Joseph's actions highlight the converse—that his pure use of his body (his earnestness to flee immorality) would honor the Lord versus sinning against Him (Gen. 39:12). David underscores as much, too—that his transgression was primarily vertical (Ps. 51:4).

So, what does one do with all that? If the sinning (through lust, with one's body) is an outright attack against God, as we use our bodies as instruments of unrighteousness (Rom. 6:13, 19), then the first relationship in need of resolution is with the Lord. From that reconciliation, every other truth must flow.

Where once we have been forgiven, where Christ has been charged with our sinning as we were propelled along by our own self-gratification and disregard for His holy standards (which were instituted for the sake of preserving and safeguarding marital intimacy), there is no further need for cleansing. For once, for all, His sacrifice appeased the justice of God (Heb. 9:26–28). In that regard, He puts aside our sinfulness with an intentional "not remembering" (Jer. 31:34; Heb. 8:12).

With that said, it is just as essential that the one receiving back someone who has committed those deeds of the flesh also go through the exercise of taking to heart what God has declared clean (Acts 10:15) by specifically "not remembering" the sins. This process is crucial and continuous, since the sin was also against him or her (in having been defrauded of what was rightfully one's own, yet spent by their spouse on another), and the remembrance of those losses will often surface, or even create a painful undercurrent in the dynamic.

It is easy (tempting, to the point of self-righteousness) to fault the one who defrauded/failed with a kind of "long memory" (versus 1 Cor. 13:5) that never sees past the uncleanness. Christ does not deal with us in this way. Instead, He counts His work utterly finished (in need of no additional atonement, no further polishing) and—cleansing us by the washing of the word (Eph. 5:26)—sees us as having "no spot … [but being] blameless" (v. 27).

For the one who is absorbing the costliness of the other's past actions, it is a matter of a deliberate (and repeated) practice every time an unforgiving spirit appears …

- **to recall the truth of Christ's work in the other believer**

    "Therefore from now on we recognize no one according to the flesh; even though we have known Christ according to the flesh, yet now we know Him in this way no longer. Therefore if anyone is in Christ, he is a new creature …" (2 Cor. 5:16–17)

- **to take the Lord at face value**

    "What God has cleansed, no longer consider unholy." (Acts 10:15)

- **to extend grace to the other by remembering that there is no "higher ground" at the foot of the cross**

    "All have sinned and fall short of the glory of God." (Rom. 3:23)

"There is none righteous, not even one … There is none who seeks for God; All have turned aside …" (Rom. 3:10–12)

"All of us like sheep have gone astray; Each of us has turned to his own way." (Isa. 53:6)

- **to recognize one's own frailty**

    "Since he himself also is beset with weakness …" (Heb. 5:2)

    "Wretched man that I am! Who will set me free from the body of this death?" (Rom. 7:24)

- **to extend a hospitable, merciful spirit—with wariness of one's own vulnerability**

    "Brethren, even if anyone is caught in any trespass, you who are spiritual, restore such a one in a spirit of gentleness; each one looking to yourself, so that you too will not be tempted." (Gal. 6:1)

- **to pray in earnest for explicit healing from the transgression, and from even the repercussions**

    "Therefore, confess your sins to one another … so that you may be healed … My brethren, if any among you strays from the truth and one turns him back, let him know that he who turns a sinner from the error of his way will save his soul from death and will cover a multitude of sins." (James 5:16, 19–20)

- **to become a proactive part of the balm—reflecting Christ's more profound welcome**

    "We had to celebrate and rejoice, for this brother of yours was dead and has begun to live, and was lost and has been found." (Luke 15:32)

- **to allow the repentant one to prove a newfound zeal for purity**

    "For behold what earnestness this very thing, this godly sorrow, has produced in you … what avenging of wrong!" (2 Cor. 7:11)

- **to forgive, again and again …**

    "Up to seventy times seven." (Matt. 18:22)

- **as God has forgiven us in Christ**

    "Be kind to one another, tender-hearted, forgiving each other, just as God in Christ also has forgiven you." (Eph. 4:32)

- **to entrust the life of the restored one to his/her Maker on an ongoing basis**

    "And now I commend you to God and to the word of His grace, which is able to build you up and to give you the inheritance among all those who are sanctified." (Acts 20:32)

- **to joy in extending a portrait of God's saving grace to us in Christ, who took back the offender with a mercy replete.**

"For it was the Father's good pleasure for all the fullness to dwell in Him, and through Him to reconcile all things to Himself, having made peace through the blood of His cross … And although you were formerly alienated and hostile in mind, engaged in evil deeds, yet He has now reconciled you in His fleshly body through death, in order to present you before Him holy and blameless and beyond reproach" (Col. 1:19–22)

To Him be the glory forever and ever, Amen!

Upfront

I have quipped before that people should come with warning labels of all the baggage they bring. It would save vast trouble compared to gradually uncovering the magnitude undisclosed to the eye. Perhaps especially visible and pointed, there seem to be at least two particular circumstances in which the fees blindside us: for one, when there has been a severe childhood trauma, and for another, when we get a glance "behind the curtain" of the spiritual bastions wreaking misery.

In children whose early years were shaped by astounding scars, the common thread seems to emerge: that, whether due to the inability to cope developmentally with inundating strains of intense melancholy and absent love or the sheer nature of our humanity to grow calloused under harsh experiences, there is an uncanny hastening of unregenerate man's maturity. It is as if the jaded element, that one would expect to materialize years down the road, reaches full bud well beyond its years; the edginess and cynicism take root and blossom at earlier seasons.

No matter how much one may tout, "We put the 'fun' in 'dysfunction,'" the ramifications of those decimating events (even to further generations) are far-reaching and repelling. When we are relating to those who have sustained such a blow, it is simple to react only to the hefty penalties of the contact, rather than delve beneath the externals. Our involvement in such times may be deterred by each staggering realization of the quagmire engulfing us.

In the other condition, as bondage on the spiritual plane becomes apparent, whether in habits or lifestyle choices, there is likewise an unpleasant discovery (perhaps in progressive intervals) over how pervasive the unhealthiness. The "hidden fees" surface as we glimpse, momentarily, the fierceness of the spiritual forces and destructive principalities that jeer, "Entice him, and see … how we may overpower him that we may bind him to afflict him" (Judges 16:5). Between the entangling ignorance and alluring iniquity, the trickery of sin (see Heb. 3:12–13; 11:25) traps and steals and loots with stealth. The cruel subtlety of bondage is that it is built on both a willful and a coerced opposition to God.

I can recall one particular instance in which my confounded cries over a beleaguered soul reached the Lord with sheer incredulity. "He *hates* You; don't You even *care?*" Immediately the Lord's dauntless paradigm, pleasing in His sight for centuries, crystallized: His care is so intense that He continues sending believers into the lives of those who have hated Him most vehemently. Saul was breathing death (Acts 9:1) when the Lord Himself "arrested" him[25] and then compelled a disquieted but persistently faithful Ananias to minister to this former persecutor of His Name (v. 10–19).

In either of the two cases, when the circumstantial or uncircumvented ailments would reckon aloof the believers who are standing by, we arrive at a flashpoint. Our decision to embrace the costliness or to evade the wreckage altogether contends with our conscience. We may be fully convinced of the worthwhile investment; we may find no difficulty identifying the fruitfulness of attending to mourners in need of a departure point. But staying engaged may be the hurdle of the hour.

For we can conjecture that distance will yield a peaceful reward (we will self-protectively exist, regardless of what the withering one needs), or we can plow directly into the fire, "having mercy on some, who are doubting; saving others, snatching them out of the fire; and on some having mercy with fear, hating even the garment polluted by the flesh" (Judges 1:22–23).

Yet the indwelling Spirit, the seal of our salvation and adoption (Rom. 8:14–16; Eph. 1:13–14), is the same who empowered Christ to declare when setting His face toward Jerusalem (Luke 9:51), "Willingly.I will sacrifice to You" (Ps. 54:6; Matt. 26:39, 42, 44). He abides in us to bring us to terms with what it means to "swear to our own hurt and not change" (Ps. 15:4).

For the Messiah who lives in us (Gal. 2:20) did not swerve in the face of sinners' hostility (Heb. 12:2–3). He enlivens our feet to tread with endurance the path carved out. He labors within us, even in birthing pangs of tedious, strained interactions, "so that when we have done the will of God, we may receive what was promised" (Heb. 10:36).

His work is unflagging (Phil. 1:6). No plan of His can be thwarted (Job 42:2; Isa. 14:27; Dan. 4:35). Even when we would recoil at the uneasiness fomented by unreasonable ways of others' relating, "His purpose will be established, and He will accomplish all His good pleasure" (Isa. 46:10).

Whether the aching soul—debilitated or defiant—is scraping hard against the one Christ has deployed for the mission, the rescue is on. In vibrant, animated, strategic means, God proves Himself invariably as the One who "does not take away life, but plans ways so that the banished one will not be cast out from Him" (2 Sam. 14:14). Through Him who stayed the full course of *our* recovery (John 19:30), we receive power (Acts 1:8) to be witnesses of Him who carried in His own Being (Isa. 53:4–6) every scrap of baggage that had sorely longed for His relief.

"Content" with Sin

A study in Paul's letter to the Romans spurred our discussion group to muse over how masterfully God saves rebels. Our facilitator wryly observed that an antagonizing and hostile spirit is "a heart that's primed for God to change!" He seems to specialize in subduing insurgents—especially since all other varieties seems to be in short supply (Rom. 3:12–18; 5:10).

And yet it is unduly tempting to speculate that those in rebellion, especially those intentionally engaged in warfare (Job 18:4; Isc. 45:9; Jer. 48:30) against the Holy Spirit (1 Thess. 4:7–8; cf 1 Sam. 8:7) and actively rejecting His call on their lives (Luke 12:10), are satisfied with the lot chiseled out for themselves—as if *un*godliness ever reaped gain (1 Tim. 6:5–6). As one fellow student of the Word noted, "Sin always over promises and under delivers."[26]

Worse yet, there comes a point—on account of sin's very nature to destroy goodness and vitality (Gen. 2:17; 4:7–8; Rom. 5:12–15; 1 John 3:12)—in which the one leveling the offense appears to exit that realm of humanity and amount to nothing more than a shell of the glorious Image he was made to reflect (Gen. 1:27–28). Sin's failure to produce the unimaginable bliss it touts (see Heb. 11:25) seems minimal in comparison to how verifiably it calluses the heart and mind

(Eph. 4:18; 1 Tim. 4:2; Heb. 3:13), and eventually dares to extinguish those vestiges of the mark of one's Creator. *Transgression degrades the human soul.*

Thus, when it becomes wickedly alluring to classify another human being into a demeaned status (which sin is already accomplishing with ardent vigor), it is then that the one with a grievance must focus his mind on the eternal soul at stake. For, although the shroud of sin's consequences may weigh heavily upon the injured spirit, yet it is absolutely vital to meditate upon the nature of the one committing the offense: that, in the case of an unbeliever, he is a soul consigned to slavery (2 Chron. 12:8; Rom. 7:14); storm-tossed, and not comforted (Isa. 54:11); spiting himself, to his own harm (Jer. 7:19; 25:6–7); filling up the measure of his guilt (Matt. 23:32), with his soul not right within him (Hab. 2:4); with his sin ever before him (Ps. 51:3); and with the Lord's hand heavy upon him (Ps. 32:4).

He is unable to detect the lie in his right hand (Isa. 44:20), unable to see, on account of the iniquities that have overtaken him (Ps. 36:1–2; 40:12), and not heard by the Lord in his praying (Ps. 66:18; Isa. 59:2; John 9:31). He lives as one with deeds not heeded by Yahweh (Isa. 58:1–5), and with no access to God's peace, loving-kindness, or compassion (Jer. 16:5). He is treated with the Lord's adversarial role (Nu. 22:32; Jer. 50:31) and under His hostility (Lev. 26:24, 41), imprisoned "in misery and chains" (Ps. 107:10), held captive by the enemy of his soul (2 Tim. 2:26; 1 Pet. 5:8), alienated from fellowship (1 John 1:6–7), and detached from his only Source of nourishment and vitality (Col. 2:19).

He has become the object of usury (Ps. 89:22), bowed down with sin (Ps. 38:3–6), fearful of man (1 Sam. 15:24;

Isa. 57:11), and mistaken in his understanding of Christ's justice (Ps. 10:13; Eccles. 8:11; Zeph. 1:12). He has been sold for his iniquities and given up for spoil (Deut. 32:30; Isa. 42:24; 50:1). He has corrupted himself (Exod. 32:7), gone deep in depravity (Hos. 9:9), and been joined to his idols (Hos. 4:17).

He is flourishing, only to be destroyed (Ps. 92:7; cf Ps. 37:9–10, 13), is set in slippery places (Deut. 32:35; Ps. 73:18), is one who has judged himself unworthy of eternal life (Acts 13:46), is a slave of corruption, is overcome (2 Pet. 2:19), is caught in destructive heresies (2 Pet. 2:1), and is unsatisfied apart from Christ, the Lord (Eccles. 2:25). He is relying upon oppression and extortion (Isa. 30:12; Jer. 22:17), mourning all day long (Ps. 38:6–8), known to the Lord as one whose "transgressions are many" and whose "sins are great" (Amos 5:12).

The one caught in the throes of sin's deceptive wages has not in truth struck upon any enamoring find but rather has spent his years with sorrow and sighing. Surrounded by a "multitude of oppressions" (Job 35:9), besieged by the haunting endeavors that chased him far from Life Himself (Luke 24:5; John 1:4; Rev. 1:18), he is woefully separated from Christ, having no hope and without God (Eph. 2:12).

And yet, we are gravely mistaken to conclude that this one, whose strength has failed because of his iniquity (Ps. 31:10), cannot be relieved of his fears through grace[27] or cannot come to value the escape route from temptation (1 Cor. 10:13) afforded by the Blood poured out from heaven's throne. For the soul who sins against us is not any less a candidate for God's wholesale interference with our "mad career of sinning"[28] than were *we*.

Bloodstained Upholstery

During one of the darker days of my bout with anorexia, my dad lovingly chided me that I could lose weight by amputation but that my quality of life probably wouldn't improve. Point taken.

Still, that isn't the only mangled perspective I have maintained. When I am absorbing an injury, my initial impulse is to dehumanize the one whose actions touch me with woe. I disregard the internal state of affairs within a fellow creature (even if unsaved) and concern myself only with the repercussions the person's status levels on me. The preoccupation is as unworthy a consideration as whether a car-wreck victim may stain the interior upholstery.

The Savior demands I perceive aright. This One, "who stretches out the heavens, lays the foundation of the earth, and forms the spirit of man within him" (Zech. 12:1), uniquely and comprehensively apprehends every overt and obscure burden, not only of our own making but also of the people who have garnered for us undeniable harm.

To alight on what He surveys entails setting aside depersonalized calculations. We are beckoned to listen more deeply, even as the King of Glory refused to deliver those shouting "Hosanna" (Matt. 21:9) in a rudimentary, superficial fashion, when the most damaged places in need of His answer were the souls ravaged by sin and alienation from their Maker (Eph. 2:12). In like manner, He produces a more profound disclosure, until we can deduce that the one who is tormenting us is himself also tormented (Isa. 54:11).

It is a supernatural perspective to stop belaboring the anguish consigned to us and to begin recognizing the hurt of the one cultivating our discomfort. That is not to say that pity and *pathos* drive us to pardon but that God Himself dealt with us as those He proactively noted to be plagued by the taskmaster of our transgression (see Exod. 3:7–8). His mercy extended itself vigorously *beyond the indecency to the individual.*

And so, whether the person whom we are striving (each hour) to forgive is willfully set against us or ignorantly accruing our injuries, we are invited to consider how the following descriptors may pair themselves with the soul we are coming to uncover as this (albeit unwelcome) set of dynamics transpires.

Especially in the case of one who is not yet enslaved to Righteousness (Rom. 6:18; Eph. 6:6) may we more readily behold the wretched predicament of one who does not yet know Him, the Source of eternal life (John 17:3), and who is subsequently not separated from the havoc and disquietude of

- humiliction
- degradation
- compulsion
- a vertical sever
- loneliness, isolation
- alienation
- shame

- bitterness
- hardness of heart
- an inability to receive from God's hand
- enslavement to the tyranny of sinfulness
- obsessions with disease-ridden thinking
- destruction
- haughtiness
- hindered prayers
- disgust in one's own behavior
- baseness of thinking and perceiving
- distrust in God's kindness
- the necessity of self-reliance in one's resources, abilities
- unresolved guilt, and embarrassment over past actions
- remorse over opportunities lost
- an impression of irrevocably "lost innocence"
- unsoundness of spirit
- uncleanness of soul
- hypocrisy
- entanglement in lies from which one cannot be freed
- the misery of "chains"
- lack of fellowship with God, or believers
- lack of guidance from His Word
- entrapment in detrimental, fatal thinking
- the inability to be "in control" or to defeat one's sins
- answering to God for profaning His Name
- disgust with one's own heedlessness
- self-hatred
- a proper expectation of punishment
- alignment with Satan's will
- darkness, hopelessness, despair

- anger at one's self, helplessness, depression
- hiding, with the fear of being "found out"
- estrangement as one seeks to conceal one's wrongs
- a seared conscience
- disconnection from truth and peace
- unrest, discontent, dissatisfaction
- strife
- confusion
- a sense of being justly abandoned by God
- the terror of being wholly unacceptable to Him
- the impossible rigidity of law-keeping
- disdain for one's own tendencies
- dual wills at play (for health and disease)
- no means of escape through one's own ingenuity
- the never-slackening accumulation of guilt
- the burning of God's anger (Exod. 32:10)
- a burdened delusion to fight for "self"
- the sway of man-centered ambition
- contempt for life's purpose
- enslavement to earthly appetites
- deadness to hope for Christ's deliverance
- the mockery over what freedom *could* have been
- the belief that one's days amount to nothing more than sins
- cognizance over creating one's own misery
- the compulsion to mask festering guilt
- an inability to detect sins
- powerlessness over regret
- the disaster one cannot "charm away" (Isa. 47:11)
- the mangled relationships (some, beyond repair)
- the weight of culpability (see Ps. 32:3–4)
- glaring pangs over irreversible damage

- languishing over having distrusted the Lord
- the inability to veil one's moral deficiency before God
- the foolishness of "turning away" from Him (Isa. 57:17)

Is it possible to peer beyond the bloodstained upholstery?

There may, Lord willing, come a moment when the person troubling our soul bows in genuine humility—eternally righteous and eagerly reverent before the God who has absolved him of all folly and guilt. But whether that day arrives, are we, as the believing party in the mix, "calling down grace"[29] upon the one who has set himself as our enemy (Luke 6:27–28)?

Although our permission to enter this person's life may come only through crossing the threshold of sorrow, our merciful Heavenly Father (Luke 6:36) imparts to His children (v. 35) the sacred right to "not return evil for evil or insult for insult, but to give a blessing instead" (1 Pet. 3:9). As those "called for the very purpose that we might inherit a blessing" (1 Pet. 3:9), we are freed to care for the state of the transgressor more than for any fallout we traverse. Empowered to serve our persecutor with diligent grace (Rom. 12:14), we bear resemblance to Christ, the Man whose unmitigated favor insisted that, when our life-breath ebbed away, His bloodstains intervened.

Compassionate Rebuke[30]

First Samuel 3:13 reads, "For ... I am about to judge (Eli's) house forever for the iniquity which he knew, because his sons brought a curse on themselves and he did not rebuke them."

The level of responsibility seems somewhat astounding. Eli's sons, Hophni and Phinehas, were—especially in their position of leadership as priests—highly accountable for their evil. Sentenced for both their defrauding of sacrifices (1 Sam. 2:12–17) and their promiscuity (v. 22), the two were slain in a single day of battle (see 1 Sam. 2:34; 4:11).

And yet, while Eli had challenged his sons ("Why do you do such ... evil things?" 2:23), still the thirteenth verse in chapter three shows that his correction availed nothing and was not even effective in terminating his accountability. His house was to be judged "for the iniquity which he knew," but "did not rebuke."

Whatever the reason, Eli's passivity proves his attitude toward sin. Had he been serious about his sons' holiness, had his utmost desire been for their sanctification, he would have "delivered those who were being taken away to death" (Prov. 24:11). Instead, he abided his sons' self-destruction.

Now, while Eli's error by no means is the reason for his sons' downfall, still, in one day, he experienced the loss of both children; he was not immune to the iniquity he had obliquely condoned. And while it is true that each servant stands or falls before his own Master (Rom. 14:4), there is also an inextricable link between those committing the transgression and the one who stands by, quietly abetting rampant corruption.

And yet, when we are bearing up under the injustices wrought by a fellow sinner's actions against us and behold in the offing one whose ambivalent eye emboldened those misdeeds, how do we portion out which areas need enveloping in our conscious action to forgive? For it is one thing to face the point-blank offense with concerted efforts to pardon yet quite another to cradle to ourselves the reality that someone allied himself nearly enough to "strengthen the hands" of the person committing the affront (see Judges 9:24). How far must our forgiveness reach?

Is it not sufficient to navigate all the volitional exercises of pardon toward the one directly responsible, that a person must also deal with the fallout born of negligence or appeasement? How do we not broil with bitterness and hostility toward those whose actions precipitated or protected the deeds now playing havoc with our daily existence? How do we process that ungodly attitude in which esteem for the one proliferating sin essentially approved the damages we sustained?

God, who came in the flesh to convert rather than condemn us (John 3:17), refuses to complacently witness our headlong rush into our demise; therefore, any complicity in a transgression serves as the antithesis of the Lord's design. Further, His Word is radically clear on how He would steer His children away from the folly of *participating* in another's wicked deeds. Second John 1 highlights the need to refrain from even greeting one who adheres to false doctrine (see v. 10–11), and Proverbs 1 instructs us to "keep from the path" of sinners who would entice and incite us to "throw in our lot" with the wicked (see Prov. 1:10–15). There is no leeway to entertain even the appearance of evil (1 Thess. 5:22).

Yet, what happens when an unbelieving crowd fails to recognize, let alone heed, those directions? What most becomes a believer when responding to non-Christians who are aiding, and perhaps even augmenting, the uneasiness we endure?

In the Psalms, David cries out, "O God, arrogant men have risen up against me, and a band of violent men have sought my life, and they have not set You before them" (Ps. 86:14). Our first response is to cry "up." We can then appeal to His true nature: "But You, O Lord, are a God merciful and gracious, slow to anger and abundant in lovingkindness and truth. Turn to me, and be gracious to me" (v. 15–16a). As those accepted in the Beloved (Eph. 1:6), we are heard by Him (see John 9:31). And we may then request His advocacy: "Show me a sign for good, that those who hate me may see it ... because You, O LORD, have helped me and comforted me" (Ps 86:16). There is no indignity in seeking God's rectification of all perspectives.

And so, while we must run the course of laying down any animosity of soul toward the one who contributed to our discomfort, we are freed (as God's bondslaves) to advance in carrying out "the will of God that by doing right we may silence the ignorance of foolish men" (1 Pet. 2:15).

Our work may not necessarily be to confront the gross compromise, but it can invariably be with the end view that honorable suffering produces a blessing (1 Pe. 3:14), provides an opportunity for our testimony of Christ (3:15), and fashions us to stand on solid ground when being unjustly reviled (3:16). Although the circumstances may not be to our choosing, still the weapons are to *His*, as He conveys us to those who are void of the proper understanding: that every sin, even the most subtle one, will find an accounting (Nu. 32:23)—either in the offender or in the One given up for our offenses.

May we recollect that, as the afflicted ones Christ has beautified with salvation (Ps. 149:4), we now inherently carry with us into every venue the dignifying mark of His effective, eternal standing. Both to the one who is "daring and self-willed" (2 Pet. 2:10), "indulging the flesh in its corrupt desires" (v. 9), and to the one who would absolve him from all censure, may we determine that our lives "preach hard—in love!"[31]

Friendly Fire

At one of my earliest birthday parties, when the fun of the hour was scampering over the sprinklers and blades of grass with a bunch of other six-year-olds, I encountered a slippery spot on the aggregate cement that left me impressed with its mark. The abrasion never made it to the bone, but it was still a fascinating study!

Even the typical first-aid course will be quick to offer classical definitions of common wounds. From punctures to avulsions, there are injuries that can be neatly categorized into symptoms and treatment options.

But there is a kind of wound most baffling. For, while we would divvy each of our spiritual aches into clean groupings, one sort defies simplistic classification. Symptomatically, it presents the same as any other injury. In treatment, it still compels us to acknowledge that nursing bitterness is like "drinking poison and expecting the other person to die."[32] It can spur us just as forcefully to seek from the Lord's storehouses the flawless justice that He, who "knows all things perfectly and exhaustively,"[33] can mete out. It can drive us to the point of "breakage," in which every visceral reaction contorts and drains us of hope, and we seek only "forgetfulness" (see Gen. 41:51). And it can generate in us the woeful spirit, which must "sob in secret for such pride" (Jer. 13:17).

Yet the cause is entirely distinct.

Unlike every other lunging, piercing, surging catalyst of pain, this variety is so definitively "other" because of its source. Oh, we are just as readily called to own the wound, not offsetting it as something outside of ourselves (as though denying it would bid it depart), but the absorption compels our heart to comprehend in full the mistakenness of the tragedy.

As David writes in Psalm 55:12–14,

> For it is not an enemy who reproaches me,
> Then I could bear it;
> Nor is it one who hates me who has exalted
> himself against me,
> Then I could hide myself from him.
> But it is you, a man my equal,
> My companion and my familiar friend;
> We who had sweet fellowship together…

Jesus was not immune to such betrayal. While Peter's flesh-reliant boast (Luke 22:33) dematerialized under threat (v. 60), the greater agony came not in the sudden moral collapse but in the fuller sweep of how everything about the relationship he had with his Lord—from the initial acquaintance to the deepening trust, from the intensity of afflictions to the depth of trials; from the unified stance to unique station apart from the majority—bonded them immensely yet seemed to disintegrate instantly for the sake of a fleeting (and worthless) trade-off in what would prove a false security.

In some cases, we discover that the years of cultivating closeness and aligning affections, the pleasantness of dwelling together in unity (Ps. 133:1), came to be snuffed out for unprincipled reasons—but not necessarily with the offending party's awareness. On occasion, the contentions are upward, and we are simply caught in the crossfire. In certain instances, the Lord is even employing such a drastic arena to captivate the attention of the one at odds with Him, as He leverages a steely reckoning with how the animosity waged vertically inherently damages loved ones on earth as well.

And yet, as the people who must claim the shrapnel of "friendly fire," the misdirected mortar shells of one who is "not an enemy," how do we fare in our comportment? Are we willing, as the letter to Philemon exhorts us, to accept him as we would accept the Lord Himself (see v. 17)? Would we dare receive to ourselves once again the one in whom we trusted, though it be the same who lifted up his heel against us (Ps. 41:9)? Are we to permit an unguarded re-entry?

Deuteronomy 10:18–19 furnishes insight. In the midst of commands defining how His people would be set apart, God offers a significant distinguishing factor when He articulates: "He ... shows His love for the alien. ... So show your love for the alien, for you were aliens in the land of Egypt." Leviticus 19:34 further elaborates, "The stranger who resides with you shall be to you as the native among you, and you shall love him as yourself, for you were aliens in the land of Egypt; I am the LORD your God." If God's response to our sin-enslavement was to love us, then our response to another's (even willful) estrangement from us is to exhibit extravagant benevolence: to shine forth with His hospitality to the hostile.

While trust is not instantly rebuilt any more than Peter could have bypassed the progression of being restored and re-commissioned (see John 20:1–21:22), still love arranges provision for the sins that will separate friends and covers those transgressions (see Prov. 10:12; James 5:20)—actively (Prov. 17:9), fervently (1 Pet. 4:8)—by preferring to welcome back rather than ward off another; desiring restoration in lieu of relegation to the past.

And in such a framework, the Lord's graciousness comes to be reflected in us as we embrace the privilege of ministering as He has to us, ensuring that we who were "separate from Christ, excluded from the commonwealth of Israel, and strangers to the covenants of promise, having no hope and without God in the world" (Eph. 2:12) are brought near by the costly Blood (v. 13) of the One who sustained our betrayal.

Our Lot in Life

Seldom would it occur to me that God sometimes locates us, much like "righteous Lot," in settings where we are intentionally distressed by others' sin. Second Peter 2:7–9 elucidates one such scenario, in which Abraham's nephew, Lot, had been "oppressed by the sensual conduct of unprincipled men" on a daily basis: "For by what he saw and heard that righteous man, while living among them, felt his righteous soul tormented day after day by their lawless deeds."

What benefit would there be in the ongoing exposure to unrighteous deeds? True, Noah stood as a preacher of the truth by his godly conduct (Heb. 11:7) and probably delivered much conviction to those who were happy eating, drinking, and marrying (see Matt. 24:38) prior to the worldwide deluge. But are the mockery and mental unrest of living in proximity worth the testimony extracted from such an aim?

Jesus's words dig in more. In Luke 11:49–50, He declares to those leaders who played at "religion" and destroyed the divinely-appointed spokespeople in their midst that God's wisdom ordained to send these messengers, "so that the blood of all the prophets, shed since the foundation of the world, may be charged against this generation." Directing His own people into grievous situations solidified an unswerving culpability for those who made themselves His adversaries.

Why does the Eternal Shepherd count fortifying a person's guilt so crucial? What advantage is there if one can look back later and proclaim that his deeds were all the more ruthless in the face of the godly man whom he harassed? What benefit is there—to anyone—when the person transmitting ungodliness and the other who must tolerate it are brought into such close quarters? Is there some reason the Lord withholds the yearned-for path of escape from one who may, with all his being, long to have "wings like a dove" so that he could "fly away and be at rest" in his "place of refuge" (Ps. 55:6, 8)?

The ramifications feel less far-fetched when paired with Christ's call to daily take up our cross in pursuit of Him (Luke 9:24). Remaining in a sphere of unrelenting crimes may well fuel our heightened dependence on the One who—promising us trouble He has vanquished (John 16:33)—delineates that our spiritual act of service is to present ourselves as "consumable matter," surrendered to the Lord's use in worshipful response to the mercies He has invested in us (Rom. 12:1). Enlivened to His pure desires, we can even clasp to ourselves the reproach (Ps. 69:7, 9; Jer. 15:15b) that adamantly identifies us as "belonged" to the One whose love has saturated our hearts (Rom. 5:5).

We also clasp anticipation. Awaiting us will be the imperishable reward reserved for those whom He upheld while being persecuted for the sake of righteousness (Matt. 5:10). Not only will our experience confirm that entry into His kingdom comes "through many tribulations," but we will also be strengthened in soul as we continue in the faith (see Acts 14:22). Any honor that we lay at the feet of the

One who has "chosen gladly" to give us His kingdom (Luke 12:32) will be accorded to us in the long term (1 Sam. 2:30), as He leads us to that "heavenly country" (Heb. 11:16), in which our reward is "well secured, out of the reach of chance, fraud, and violence."[34]

Yet, if self-denial and satisfaction apart from this world are shaping us to appreciate the conformity (Rom. 8:29) and comfort (Rev. 14:12–13) for which our hearts were genuinely designed, then what is being wrought in the heart of an unbeliever who cradles to himself the hostile raging of having "deeply defected" (Isa. 31:6) from the Holy One? Is there any good effect on the man who has, as his heartbeat, a rich disdain toward "whatever is true, right, and pure" (Phil. 4:8)?

Perhaps we can draw from the Lord's dealings with Israel, as His people, stationed in Goshen, awaited final deliverance from centuries of Egyptian bondage. It was not until the fourth of ten plagues that the Lord started to make a distinction (Exod. 8:22–23) between the pagan slaveholders and the monotheistic, nearly freed slaves. While it is true that God sends His rain on the just and the unjust (Matt. 5:45), there may be times when He illustrates the favor distinctly reserved for those who know Him in the full scope of His redemption; who understand Him to be Sustainer, but who have come to learn Him personally as Savior (see 1 Tim. 4:10). We may be in near range to one who is venomous because it behooves the person to see the spectrum of care the Lord would likewise pour upon him, if he were but willing (see Matt. 23:37; cf Ps. 81:13–14; 84:11–12).

And in still other instances, it may be that, where the callousness of another increases, it is only that we might finally learn to pray. In one season, when my "lot in life" began making readily evident that I was interacting with one plagued by guilt, any provocation took on a new context: I was only involved in the peripheral sense. Much as a believer may perceive himself to be on the receiving end of an unbeliever's explicit angst, ours is not the commandment that has been trampled (see Gen. 2:17; Exod. 20:1–17). Ours is not the covenant transgressed (see Judges 2:20). And ours is not the created order that has come under attack through haughty self-centeredness (see Isa. 14:13–14). God alone owns His creatures (Ezek. 18:4), and none evades accountability to Him (2 Chron. 6:23; Rom. 14:10, 12; Heb. 9:27; cf Rev. 2:23). It may simply be that we have been brought in on the verge of a judgment that God will dispense at a suitable hour. But in any case, the interplay emblazons our prayers.

For from that peeled-back vantage point, we can—even as we scrape up against another's sinful behavior—begin to lament the violation of the Lord's precious law (Ps. 119:136) and intercede more vigorously over the vertical rupture (Ps. 51:4; Isa. 59:2; Lam. 2:1). For the bulk of the matter deals with His being despised (see 1 Sam. 2:29), disregarded (see Isa. 22:11b), and defamed (Ezek. 36:22), while we are simply in the way. Aye, strategically placed "in the way" but not the primary cause when the key issue hinges upon God's relationship with the wayward one.

In a strangely comforting way, there is even relief to learn that, although such placement may be enigmatic while we traverse the hostility, God is revealing His perspective on grievous factors we could never otherwise distinguish: distilling for our eyes' discovery that the spirit alongside us has been willing to forfeit his eternal well-being (Matt. 16:26). Blinded by crushing lawlessness, he has failed to value the One of supreme worth (1 Tim. 1:17; 6:15–16; cf 1 Pet. 1:19) and still has hanging over him the penalties of all those who are rebels of Christ (John 3:36).

When we step back momentarily to ascertain the principalities at war (Eph. 6:12), as strangleholds and strongholds wreak their destruction on souls incited to curse the only One good, we understand that we have been subjected to nothing more than a fellow sinner's shameless deeds. Outright attack is reserved for the King of Glory. May we ever bind ourselves in petition to Him who has "words of eternal life" (John 6:66–68), so that those who assault Righteousness Himself may—in having their speculations torn down by divinely powerful weapons of the believers' warfare (2 Cor. 10:4–5)—cease the striving that spurns His exaltation (Ps. 48:10).

Crying Out

I saw underneath the altar the souls of those who had been slain because of the word of God, and because of the testimony which they had maintained; and they cried out with a loud voice, saying, "How long, O Lord, holy and true, will You refrain from judging and avenging our blood?"

—Revelation 6:9–10

Singing in the Dark[35]

Roughly two weeks after all my world came crashing down, I attended a youth conference in the place that my nourishing Redeemer (Rev. 12:6) would later designate as my "place of refuge" (Ps. 55:8). As our group was returning to the convention hall, where the final stretch of workshop sessions would conclude the three-day event, there was room enough in the van for all but one. I remained on the church campus where we had been lodging and, awaiting the return of the driver, gained in the frosty morning air a few moments for the contemplation that had been failing to happen while amidst the crew of teenagers with whom I had traveled.

There was an insufficient connection. Trying to force a "wiring" between what my eyes had recently witnessed and what my gut kept shrieking was wrong, I possessed no ability to bridge the glaring chasm. Words faintly rose, with disbelief spewing out in fretful bursts, but friends could only watch as I sat in a distant land of inconsolability. I was not in need of phrases that might have fallen from their lips; I simply wanted reassurance that others stood with me in taking this new paradigm as a jarring, irreconcilable blast that seemed harshly imposed and sorely in need of dismissal. Helpless, I lingered in the quietude.

That December morning, shortly into the daylight hours,

I was gifted with a treasure that could not have been received apart from those mournful bounds. It was as I waited, leaning into the desperation but still cleaving hard to the nature of the One who was guiding me, that my voice was graced with opportunity in that deserted parking lot to raise a song of praise to the One who is eternally worthy and whom angels ceaselessly adore. In that hymn of exaltation, the darkness lifted.

Circumstances were as tainted as ever, and the ramifications would have years' worth of devastation to wreak upon my soul, but the moment I could fix my gaze aright—or rather, the instant the Lord drew me out of my downward, clouded vision—the true Priority settled the matter. Psalm 42:8 depicts well, "The LORD will command His lovingkindness in the daytime; and His song will be with me in the night, a prayer to the God of my life."

In the days thereafter, when I winced over the heaving losses, there would be instances where the pulsing, rallying cry would be of His faithfulness set to melodies that came with soul-scorching lines. Engrained and emphatic, the tunes that battered down on me and welled up through me were those testifying to His fidelity as Anchor. At other hours, a whispered refrain was all I could muster, scarcely overcoming the chokehold of emotion that stymied my voice.

By His graciously vesting me with a diminishment of all I had prior retained, He granted me confirmation that any burgeoning adoration of Him was not predicated on the quantifiable measures I would have utilized prior. Instead, as I was extracted from my former ideals, it was His intention that I cease viewing myself as a receptacle to be filled by a heavenly hand, and begin comprehending that I am an individual before my Creator, Savior, and Stay—a being in whom the Infinite has taken meticulous and tender interest, and that He only bestows upon me—in the giving or withholding (see Job 1:21)—exactly what He deems suitable to the shaping of this soul. More succinctly, He was communicating that His love was based not on that which lay in my hands but on His circumventing the nails from ever *entering* my hands. My worship could be rooted in the same.

It is discordant to think praise at its finest is offered void of stumbling blocks. We will assuredly weave in and out of daunting struggles, much as our Lord did when He walked this earth as "a man of sorrows and acquainted with grief" (Isa. 53:3). Yet, praise explodes on a heightened plane of validity when proffered to our Maker without contingencies upon anything apart from His character.

Worship is not yielded only from a grateful, peace-filled, abundantly satisfied heart. It can likewise arise (and perhaps in more concentrated, effervescent forms) from a bludgeoned, disquieted spirit. It is not necessarily a negative, or even a poor reflection, regarding the Object of our love that a firm resolution to "praise Him yet more and more" (Ps. 71:14) must be forged in the midst of broken dreams, crushed longings, unfulfilled expectancy, wearying discouragement, inundating attack, or simple exhaustion, which would all entice us to curse God to His face (Job 1:11; 2:5).

Sometimes it is precisely when every hindrance would arrest our proclamation of God's goodness that the true essence and motives of our worship are proved—that the degree, authenticity, and legitimacy of His being exalted in our lives come to the fore (Hab. 3:17–18), with no reservation concerning the One to whom reverent awe is due (Jer. 10:7).

For when neither the weariness of our prayers nor the wounded-ness of our spirit can temper our adoration of the Son of Man, then—unfettered by pretenses—our worship emerges as a "deliberate confidence"[36] in Him who bled for us. No longer constrained by concerns over less weighty issues in need of resolution, we apprehend the primary cure according to the value it possesses. Or, as the psalmist cries out with hearty declaration: "My lips will shout for joy when I sing praises to You; and my soul, which You have redeemed" (Ps. 71:23).

The Action Prevented

The Enemy's warfare is crafty but limited.[37] Tirelessly destructive and eager to avenge himself on his Maker, the Adversary revels in dismantling a man's dignity, dragging him through the filth of transgression and then crumpling him with the gnawing weight of guilt. His goals are ruthless, heartless, and incessantly vile.

Perhaps one of his shrewdest techniques actually appears quite benign at first blush, entirely unsurprising for one who guises himself as "an angel of light" (2 Cor. 11:14). He devises treacherous methods of keeping us in limbo over whether our Father's forgiveness is final, all the while dragging us into spiritual stagnancy when we could be putting our hand to the productive work of demonstrating such mercy to other desperate sinners.

Christ's merit (1 Cor. 1:30; Titus 3:5) is our release from culpability, and His life is our only appeal before Justice's bench (1 John 2:1). So long as we are waging war against lies over the veracity of His unshakeable gift, we are expending energies fruitlessly as we plateau on the mere "accomplishment" of recuperating trust.

When we are instead grounded in the deeply assuring knowledge that His righteousness abides forever and His salvation extends to all generations (see Isa. 51:8), we operate with the rational understanding that "everything He does is right and all His ways are just" (Dan. 4:37; NIV). Only then can we delve more fully into the purpose for which we were created: to be fruitful and multiply disciples in His kingdom (Matt. 28:19–20) as the exquisite nature of His reconciling love on display (John 13:34–35; 15:9–13) seizes others' regard and reverence.

Yet we do not arrive at that place of tearing into the Enemy's realm, of capturing souls for Christ, by arming ourselves with meager platitudes. Shored up with the truth of His Word, we fight tenaciously. Once we are resolved that our hardships are *for refining, not for retribution*—that our circumstances are not "bringing our iniquity to remembrance" (1 Kings 17:18), but fall under the framework of His mercifully remembering our sins "no more" (Jer. 31:34; Heb. 8:12)— we can then stride freely into our designated roles.

For we recognize that His call to this trial is not unique. Peter exhorts early (and all) believers to remember that not only is the "fiery ordeal" to be expected (1 Pet. 4:12), but it is also a common experience among the brethren (5:9). We are being proved as those whose earnest desire is to live for godliness (2 Tim. 3:12), because we are in the service of Christ Jesus (2:3).

Added to that pride-lumbering recognition, whereby we gladly accept whatever He brings to bear—even "the arrows of the Almighty" (Job 6:4), which come from His righteous hand (Job 36:3)—our submission to His royal pattern quells the agitation of our heart in recognition that He deals justly. "Lo, God will not reject a man of integrity, nor will He support the evildoers" (Job 8:20). He rejoices over His servants (Isa. 65:13–14) and will reveal through His judgments (Isa. 26:9) a joyous occasion for the righteous (Prov. 21:15).

Yet there comes the grace-soaked reminder as well that, both in our entering with Him into hardship and waiting on His avenging, He is remembering every price in the labor. We need not restlessly strive in wonder over whether He has noted the tears; we are assured that "whatever good thing done as to the Lord" will be received back from Him (Eph. 6:7–8).

We are beckoned to "not lose heart in doing good" but to hold out for the harvest (Gal. 6:9). Even when the profit of the way may be veiled to our vision, let us not revert to the slanderous conclusions that God is unjust or unmindful. Rather, let us guard vehemently the foundational truth that our Sovereign faithfully brings to pass all He has ordained (1 Thess. 5:24) and just as emphatically decrees over both His people and His purpose: "It is I who answer and look after you ... From Me comes your fruit" (Hos. 14:8).

As the early Messianic believers were exhorted to show diligence, may we likewise "realize the full assurance of hope" (Heb. 6:11) as we work the works of Him who sent Christ (John 9:4). May we especially be consoled by the lie-deconstructing reality that the God we serve is the God who sees (Gen. 16:13; 2 Chron. 16:9): "For God is not unjust so as to forget your work and the love which you have shown toward His name, in having ministered and in still ministering to the saints" (Heb. 6:10).

Successfully Submitted

A wry smile crept across my face with the confirmation of my online book order: "Successfully submitted." Fairly ironic, when the books I had ordered (about submitting to authority) attested to the fact that success never comes with a simple "click."

Still, as I grapple with the issue (primarily during my waking hours!), I can gratefully say that God has provided "ammo," for the right hand and the left (2 Cor. 6:7), which renews my perspective. He penetrates the heartbeat of deceptions through His piercing Word (Heb. 4:12).

When I implore God to explain Himself, Job 33:13 extols His immunity from human demands: "Why do you complain against Him that He does not give an account of all His doings?" When I grumble against His plans, Lamentations 3:39 supersedes my protests with a prompt rectification: "Why should any living mortal, or any man, offer complaint in view of his sins?" When I forget how my relationship with Him was resumed, and on what terms, the salient musing approaches me: "How far less the greatest afflictions that we meet with in this world … than we have deserved"[38] (see also Rom. 3:19–20; Eph. 2:3). And when I mistake myself as properly obliged to none but myself, the haunting recalibration of 1 Corinthians 6:19 vanquishes every misperception rooting sufficiency or ownership internally: "Do you not know … that you are not your own?"

Submitting is a mixture of both love and death—love for the one to whom submission is given and death to the flesh and every self-preserving stance. The seemingly incongruous elements marking devotion steer us unexpectedly into our purpose.

While the Master Architect had taken occasion before to progressively shift my suspicious demands to trusting submission, in one particular time of prayer, He suddenly and graciously elevated my perspective of His treatment of the circumstances. In that hour, weeping gave way to worship as He tenderly unraveled prior fallacies that had prevented my beholding how...

1. He was not punishing faithfulness to Him with anguish. The situation surrounding me was not an indication that He had undertaken retaliation (see 1 Kings 17:18) but rather that—as one already pardoned and claimed by Him—I was employed to "go and bear fruit" (John 15:16) in just such a scenario. Since I was not *bereft* of forgiveness but *bequeathed* it, the predicament in which I stood had everything to do with His further deploying a "servant of Christ and steward of the mysteries of God" (1 Cor. 4:1). Even from a very shallow viewpoint, it was enough to recognize that what I experienced was intended for consecration, not condemnation (Rom. 8:1).
2. He was not passively "letting" a less-than-ideal paradigm unfold. He was not wringing His hands, wondering how this turn of events had "gotten away from Him," and heading back to the drawing board

for second rate solutions! The events unraveling before me comprised the Lord's perfectly scheduled, flawlessly engineered working. With the objectives hidden from my eyes, I might have unsuccessfully squared the reason for such an outworking, but the God whom I serve "is unique and who can turn Him? And what His soul desires, that He does. For He performs what is appointed for me, and many such decrees are with Him" (Job 23:13–14).

3. He was not fashioning a crude "recovery" plan for enduring health. By His "predetermined plan and foreknowledge" (Acts 2:23), He coordinated the most hideous atrocity in all of human history for the sake of revealing that death could not constrain His Son (v. 24) and that sinful man could savor lasting hope in Him (v. 26). God has no use for a "plan B."

Much as it might appeal to the human intellect to conjecture that there were far more preferable (e.g., cleaner, less taxing, more agreeable) methods of reaching the Father's goal of spiritual regeneration and vitality, God has never been about recoiling and recuperating. His Son, slain from the foundation of the world, was the original intent carried through (Rev. 13:8), as an act of His grace, which was "granted us in Christ Jesus from all eternity" (2 Tim. 1:9).

Instead, God is at His work, always (John 5:17)—*passionately arranging His children's highest good through the only means possible to secure it!* He has forever been the One who is *most* concerned, and whose capable hands and competent heart strategically orchestrate every interaction and interlude to His pleasing (Ps. 135:6). He not only possesses the insight and foresight to weave together all things comprehensively for the execution of His good will, but—underlying His skillfulness—He is moved by "pity without end"[39] to bring about life abundant (John 10:10; 15:11).

As Charles Spurgeon[40] aptly noted,

> Remember this, had any other condition been better for you than the one in which you are, divine love would have put you there. ... Be content with such things as you have, since the Lord has ordered all things for your good. Take up your own daily cross; it is the burden best suited for your shoulder, and will prove most effective to make you perfect in every good word and work to the glory of God.

The One who "visited us and accomplished redemption for His people" (Luke 1:68) has demonstrated His unsearchable judgements and unfathomable ways (Rom. 11:33). Proactive, creative, and selfless, the Spirit of the Lord commandeered what had vanquished us and gifted us with renewal—before we drew our first breath. If His zeal performed our deliverance, how can He not be relied upon to meticulously time, flawlessly coordinate, and generously infuse with purpose His every lesser dealing with us? For the sake of Him who emptied Himself on our behalf, may we expend ourselves in testifying how "He has done all things well" (Mk. 7:37).

Placid Tumult

More than a walk but scarcely worth a drive from here, there is lovely, gushing flow of water that reminds me of how faulty my vision is. It is not because I had eye surgery when I was six—though I have more than once been reprimanded for being a licensed driver without depth perception! Instead the dilemma originates with the pool that sits adjacent, which has the most deceptive aspect of stillness. On the one side, gallons of liquid come penetrating through three small canals, tumultuously crashing against the concrete underlay and blasting at an upward trajectory to froth downstream. On the other side, with mirror-like reflection of the almond blossom trees just sneaking into spring, a glassy, flat panorama pervades. To *see* the tranquility and *hear* the cacophony is enough to ratchet one's senses into helpless defeat.

And yet it is humbling to square with one's own deficiencies. For, while it looks as though there is no movement, the splashing just beneath the bridge well confirms the exhaustively raucous activity, no matter how undetectable. That is God's movement: wild and cascading and, sadly, often eluding our every perception.

We know, as Jesus explained in John 5:17, "My Father is working until now, and I Myself am working." How easily we lose our bearings. Though we know Him to "neither slumber nor sleep" (Ps. 121:4), how readily we can fall prey to the notion that, without any outward evidence of His championing our cause in this particular hour, perhaps we are forgotten, or maybe God is unjust so as to overlook what has been done in His Name. Hebrews 6:10 counters such fallacy. He disregards nothing; our Father sees what is done in secret and will reward accordingly (Matt. 6:4, 6, 18).

Perhaps worse yet is our succumbing to the falsehood that, if we are not being neglected by the Almighty God, then we are being specifically targeted. When all looks as if He has cast us off, it is troubling enough; but when it appears that He was willfully rejected us or has set us into harsh circumstances for our deliberate undoing, it is a more taxing fight. While Scripture has the full prerogative and capacity to permeate and right our thinking, we are enlisted in the battle to assert that His Word will ultimately reconcile the "placid tumult" of events that shout a bleak contradiction to His divine love.

Our holy obligation is to believe in the dark what we have learned in the light.[41] Isaiah 49:15 emphatically highlights, "Can a woman forget her nursing child and have no compassion on the son of her womb? Even these may forget, but I will not forget you." He deals tenderly, no matter how faltering our senses may be to ascertain that "His mercies are over all His works" (Ps. 145:9).

And so, especially when we have been called in for "special ops" work, where our Commanding Officer stations us in a high intensity field of interactions with those who are unsaved and are lashing out vertically (though we receive the shrapnel horizontally), it is crucial that we absorb the truth of His mindfulness. If we are tucked into His aims of evangelizing the lost, He has made us a precious mouthpiece of His kindness and reconciliation. The One "from whom our frame was not hidden when we were made in secret, and skillfully wrought in the depths of the earth" (Ps. 139:15) knows our every ordeal on the battleground.

Equally vital is our remembrance of His outcomes. Our "lending" is essentially not to man: we are freed "with good will (to) render service, as to the Lord … knowing that whatever good thing each one does, this he will receive back from the Lord" (Eph. 6:7–8). Much as our propensity is to seek repayment from human hands, we serve as "slaves of Christ, doing the will of God from the heart" (v. 6).

And there will be a reward for our work (2 Chron. 15:7; Col. 3:24). The labor is not in vain (Phil. 2:16). We may enjoy no evidence, no sight whatsoever, but the closing harvest depends on Him who "causes the growth" (1 Cor. 3:7). He alone can "gather fruit for life eternal" (John 4:36); we are simply His co-laborers (1 Cor. 3:9; 2 Cor. 6:1).

By the power of His indwelling Spirit, who raises the dead to life (John 3:5–8), we are able to persist in a defiant faith that "walks against the signs." When the serene surface beckons us to distrust His activity, when all appears deadened in action and His hand would appear slack, when we stumble to recall the promises He has initiated on our behalf, we are graciously being permitted to grow, not in apathy and dejection "but the kind of faith God prizes (that) always looks foolish. It searches for explanations consistent with God's faithfulness."[42]

Even when stillness is all one can see.

Anti-Septic

"Going septic" was an odd phrase the first time it hit my ears. The thought of an untreated infection creating such internal toxicity as to take a sudden deadly turn stunned me.

Too many times I have been there *spiritually*. The symptoms are nothing like what Mayo Clinic reports, with increased heart rate, breathing, and body temperature—but the effect is just as deadly. Primary causes typically revolve around (1) recalling the initial injury or injustice, (2) identifying the helplessness within, (3) detecting divergences between life's prior direction and its current one in relation to sin's intrusive presence, and (4) imputing to the Lord the unfounded allegation that only by His rectifying prevailing circumstances could my belief in His care be fortified. While the first three musings bear no intrinsic harm, the concluding sentiment, brought on by a willful neglect to eliminate the poisons, causes me to walk around with a "low-grade fever."

But the Holy Spirit, steadfast to alert me when sepsis is setting in, underscores how the lame, perfunctory efforts to dismiss another's sin—by my foolishly squinting at the misdeeds to evade the full import or cavalierly dismissing life's currently misshapen form—are undermining a solacing trust in Him. Having merely deflected the gritty work of submitting the offense beneath His righteous character and designs, I have accomplished nothing but a lethal buildup.

And in that moment, He implores strict recalibration: an engagement of volition to distinctly set the offender at liberty from the framework of offense. Even if the meager starting point is composed of rote decisions, and every tattered expression of prayer begins with the stilted, "I choose to forgive," yet the willful act to absolve the transgressor as I have been acquitted (2 Cor. 5:19; Eph. 4:32) somehow becomes the glorious "letting" of the fatal fluids lodged internally. Flung across the journal pages may be line after crazed line cataloging specific indecencies and injustices (perceived and pent up), but the practice is enough to start the flow, until rawness eventually culminates in a vehement surge that pronounces the extent of the turbidity within.

Mysteriously, as the poisons surface, the locus of the reeling shifts. My eyes are no longer riveted on the hardships I have been served but on the hideous cruelties of which I am equally guilty—the brazenness and brashness, the boasting and belittling, the brandishing of my own "rights" over anyone else's—until the devastating truth crashes in: "It is all level ground before the cross."

For the devil's scheme is to turn our eyes from our own savagery (Ps. 73:21–22) until we dwell on another's, and languish under the caustic nature of an unforgiving spirit (see 2 Cor. 2:10–11; Eph. 4:26–27). Yet, as one pilgrim has astutely observed, "My wise and sovereign God takes one form of evil—my suffering—and turns it on its head to defeat an even worse evil—my sin and self-centeredness."[43] Any hardship entrusted to us, particularly any fallout from another's sin, is reaping a more acute awareness of how we have pierced our Savior.

For which soul could assert to his having committed lesser offenses against the Pure and Spotless One? And who could declare himself excused from his part in the bludgeoned body of Christ, who placed Himself (John 10:17–18) under the mocking scorn, lashing whip, pressing thorn, lacerating nail, and, more, the inundating wrath of His Father and the crushing hatred of every son of Adam?

This God, who bled for the immoral and unruly ones set on undoing His kingdom (Luke 19:14); this Man, who would elevate to heaven (John 14:2–3; Eph. 2:6; Col. 3:1) the murderous ones intent on His being silenced, intervened—with ravaged breath on an execution device; with riddled cries of abandonment (Ps. 22:1)—though He had come with precisely this mission to fulfill (Matt. 16:21; 20:28).

His crowning work—of being "horrifically suspended in between heaven and earth"—declared both the "vileness of man's sin and humanity's great unworthiness" as well as how supremely He loves us to have instituted this scene on behalf of the very ones who committed the sins necessitating it.[44]

No matter the fiercest assailing we undergo, our surest "anti-septic" is in a penetrating glimpse at the cross—the place where we, *not* the Prince of Glory, deserved to perish. As one enduring hymn laments with agonizing praise,

> Mine, mine was the transgression,
> but Thine the deadly pain.
> Lo, here I fall, my Savior!
> 'Tis I deserve Thy place …
> O make me Thine forever;
> and should I fainting be,
> Lord, let me never, never
> outlive my love to Thee … [45]

"Let Them Ask Me"

> In my distress I called upon the LORD,
> And cried to my God for help;
> He heard my voice out of His temple,
> And my cry for help before Him came into
> His ears.
> —Psalm 18:6

The novel I never published was encapsulated by this verse. The draft was actually a response to a ninth-grade writing prompt: to devise an historical fiction of under ten pages. Once the assignment was submitted, roughly 490 more pages toppled in. Somehow, "short" story was lost to me as the characters sprang to resounding life—the lead being a schoolteacher in a small Pennsylvania town, whose witnessing the conscription of her Union soldier husband carved out raw dependency on the Lord that permitted her to firmly avow to His being her solitary hope.

The verse from Psalm 18:6 seemed vaguely comforting as page after page enthusiastically spilled forth, and I fleshed out the homey community while simultaneously meandering through alternative endings. Yet the disturbing part, which perhaps I hadn't the wherewithal to articulate then, was that "reaching up" became the central focus. I was glad of the Lord's willingness to hear, but His distance (His seeming aloof, "in His temple") still portrayed a mildly estranged Deity who could not be disturbed except for major trials—military enlistments, for example.

How I neglected the valuable Incarnation! How I failed to distinguish that, amply so, He is ready to hear our prayers, but what paleness that scratches in comparison to His having come as "flesh dwelling among us" (John 1:14)! He was not, as I erroneously figured, one who refrained from involvement but One who was more dismayed (Ezek. 18:23, 32; Hos. 11:8; Zech. 1:3) over our damnation than we (see Prov. 7:23) and who aggressively moved to forfeit heaven's graces in order to rectify what we had set amiss. How He is the God who "brings near His righteousness" (Isa. 46:13)!

He stretched out His hands to a people who were not seeking Him (Isa. 65:1-2); He availed Himself to those who were not waiting on His deliverance and had already decreed it hopeless to expect any good to come (Jer. 18:12). He set His affections (Jer. 31:3; Hos. 11:4) on unresponsive ones who failed to acknowledge that it was He who had healed them (v. 3). He was actively orchestrating the wellbeing of those who could not discern how He would restore them with health and peace and truth (Jer. 33:6).

In light of such luxurious availability to His people, Ezekiel 36:37 then becomes all the more fascinating—"Thus says the Lord GOD, 'This also I will let the house of Israel ask Me to do for them'"—because in it we glimpse how much more intent the Lord is on bestowing than we are on receiving. He, in His autonomy, released His hands of the most pronounced favor He could bestow (Rom. 8:32). We, for our part, fail to ask; or, when we do, we petition with motives that betray our selfish spending (James 4:2–3) and stifle our humble dependency on the One who solves our need.

Yet what is truly intriguing, even beyond His offer to be entreated, is that He would hear us at all. As the healed man in John recounted to those who ought to have been his spiritual leaders: "We know that God does not hear sinners" (9:31). As Isaiah corroborates, "Your iniquities have made a separation between you and your God, and your sins have hidden His face from you so that He does not hear" (59:2). The psalmist also noted that our harboring any wickedness would leave a breach in our relationship with God Most High (Ps. 66:18).

Do we truly grasp? He is the offended Deity; we are the intruders. He is the Holy Law-Giver; we are despisers of the same. He had every reason to hold us aloof, punish us wholesale, and shed our blood for the sake of repayment for His broken statutes. Yet His character has not precluded Him from tendering to us mercies rich (Eph. 2:4) and unfailing (Lam. 3:22), which cause us to appreciate more of the One who is beckoning us to request.

For, if He would incite us to pray; if any offer at all of communion with Him could stand, then it must be because all resolution has been created and satisfied in Him only. Persisting for the whole of eternity, through the Savior who is "able ... to save forever those who draw near to God through Him" (Heb. 7:25), our once-tainted history has been completely rewritten. Jesus Himself has become the culmination, the utter fulfillment of the Law of righteousness, for all who believe in Him (Rom. 10:4). Without any need to make further offering for sin—since now "there is forgiveness of these things" in Him (Heb. 10:18)—we are dealt with according to His merit, and able to lift our prayers to the Father who loves us (see John 16:26–27).

If we truly grasped that communing with God in prayer is an overflow of His willfully reconciling us to Himself; an outworking of His mission to "blot out our transgressions" (Ps. 51:1) and make us "as white as snow" (Isa. 1:18), then perhaps we could come to value more intensely the treasure—not just of our communication with Him who is seated above the heavens and into whose presence His Son has granted our admittance (Heb. 4:14–16) but also of our consecration from this One who would let His people "know" Him (see Jer. 31:34)—the Healer of their sins.

Restored to His original intent for our existence (see Isa. 43:7, 21), may we tirelessly joy in the fact that His attending to our prayer is evidence of the grace in which we stand (Rom. 5:2). Where we question our true forgiveness, where we entertain thoughts that He would respond to us with reluctance, may we refocus our souls on how willfully He vested us with His righteous robes (Isa. 61:10). And from that focal point, let us be centered on the One whom we are pressing on to know (Hos. 6:3), until we then—with unbridled reassurance—proclaim of Him boldly, "Blessed be God, who has not turned away my prayer nor His lovingkindness from me" (Ps. 66:20)!

Peering Past[46]

Among the celebrations marking the close of the academic year, an inevitable glut of field trips cropped up during the final week on the calendar. Upon arrival at the recycling center, where one of my third grader's parents worked, a second-grade child in this multi-age assortment of ready-to-be-done-for-the-year students distinguished herself with uncharacteristically undisciplined behavior. I was inclined to write off the disturbances as related more to the disrupted routines than to anything specifically needing addressing. However, the incidents, growing in intensity, began bordering on dangerous, as she instigated chases, tested the volume of her lungs, and draped herself across any nearby student she could distract—all while our little gathering navigated around the heavy equipment of the facility.

Her mother, who accompanied us for the event, furnished several comments to redirect her youngster, but this little one, probably the most diminutive in the class, invented ways to insert herself in others' body space and present some overall safety issues if not restrained.

After an intermittent series of the girl's outbursts, the mother knelt on the asphalt, scooped her child close, and whispered hardly a few words to this one who had appeared, from the day's start, to be a bundle of turmoil.

The mother's demeanor gave no indication of threat or disapproval, but sufficient was the statement to crumple this tiny eight-year-old.

As cognizant onlookers turned their attention from the parent guide, leading the tour, to the heap of tearfulness collapsed inside her mother's compassionate arms, the parent, with utter dignity, assured the curious classmates and accompanying parents that the incident was in no way related to the day's event: that what un-riveted this little one was "her problem."

The extreme tenderness in concealing the reason for her daughter's weeping, and the equally intimate knowledge in addressing the internal battle within her child, only enhanced the gravity of whatever meager words were offered in correction sheer moments before. To have cut so concisely to the heart denoted pure attentiveness on the part of this parent.

I doubt such discernment and sensitivity would have struck me with such poignancy—except that God had not let me leave the house that morning without having dealt with me in like manner. After my having spent the better part of the previous night "throwing fits" and forging increasingly more recalcitrant bastions of distrust toward my Heavenly Father, in the morning, I found a rush of venom hastening forth—until His whisper suddenly brought me to shuddering tears. His piercing understanding of me well detected the cause and immediately unfastened the hurt that lay behind my raging. His gentle dealings shattered me in an instant, rendering me unable to do more than crumple, broken, in His arms.

I am unaware how He can "unwrap" me with such ease, how He pinpoints in that quiet moment the real concern wedging me from a faith-filled trust in Him, or why He would even stave off others who, with curiosity, could not resonate with all He apprehends. I only know that my Father, the One upon whom my tears are shed, is faithful, kind, and wise. And I know that, in His dealings with me, He peers past the outburst to comfort the ache behind it.

> "How deep the Father's love for us,
> how vast beyond all measure..."[47]

Remembering Christ

Should you not also have had mercy on your fellow slave, in the same way that I had mercy on you?

—Matthew 18:33

"Forgettery"

An adoptive grandma used to joke that her "forgettery" was much better than her memory! How I have yearned at times to say the same!

Joseph, whose life is showcased prominently throughout the latter portion of Genesis, draws up from the wells of my being the longing for such erasure of troubling times. The fact that this God-fearing man—bartered away as nothing better than chattel by envious and murderous kin (Gen. 37:4, 5, 18, 28), maligned and convicted of impurity which he specifically sought to avoid in reverence for his God (Gen. 39:9, 20)—should deliberately name his firstborn in line with his former adversity speaks volumes. With years' worth of untended wounds, his eldest child became the emblematic portion and declaration of the Almighty's intent: making Joseph to forget all his troubles and his father's household ("Manasseh"; Gen. 41:51).

While each person may alight upon at least one day that would undoubtedly rank most deserving of being "deleted from recall"—that moment of agonizing shattering, which burst everything inside; the disillusionment finally touching the core—that which burdened me came from an unlikely source, at a totally disconcerting instant. The "friendly fire," coming from one with whom I had taken sweet counsel (Ps.

55:12–14), erupted while defenses were down. Without my foreseeing such an occasion, the unnerving truth was at that hour plunged into my marrow: while other sins can reside in the impersonal realm of indecency or broken propriety, betrayal has a face.[48]

The difficulty arose in my absorbing how the intense memories, once comforting, now swirled in muted array around an affront so piercing that all was confirmed "unsafe." The riddle staring back at me arrived not simply in the overthrow of my expectation, but in the strangeness over how the toppling was incited by a familiar hand. The Cheshire grin, with its unspoken assertion that I could be sidestepped in attaining goals, splayed my heart with an enigmatic intrusion—enough to incite a nearly corporeal reaction. Even to this day, were there any memory I would elect first to enter my "forgettery," that look of illicit satisfaction would invariably suffice.

And yet, quite possibly, there is more at play in the heavenly places (Eph. 6:12) than I realize when considering those indelible sights we would obliterate from our consciousness. For Christ Himself—knowing the plaguing injustice of being exchanged for a paltry fee (Zech. 11:12–13; *cf* Matt. 26:15)—dwelt in the searing brutality of His being abandoned by those who had affirmed complete allegiance to Him (Matt. 26:33, 35; 56). The Gentle Shepherd, who could have called down legions of armies (Matt. 26:53) He Himself had created (Col. 1:16–17), condescended to experiencing that look: a moment of deepest interchange in which the failed loyalty of a loved one was tumultuously reaping His near demise, through a cowardly action that could not be rescinded but played instrumentally into the most gruesome hardship to be leveled on the innocent One.

In Peter's case, the recognition of bloodstained hands and deflated pomp came immediately (Luke 22:61). In other cases, it may take years for a sin to be uncovered as the solemn trespass it is (1 Tim. 5:24–25). Regardless of the timeframe, a child of the Redeeming King possesses in his or her hands the immediate *privilege, prerogative, and power* to forgive—without any dependency on the other's reaction.

What a marvelous truth, especially to those overpowered and overrun! We are not constrained to wait on communication from one who can finally repent with genuine remorse, an adequate apology, and a self-effacing stance of horror at the atrocities railed against us. Rather, when we ought to have been consigned to an "unforgivable" state for the duration of our immortal existence—as we rightfully belonged under the defensible wrath of our Holy God (Ps. 5:4; Hab. 1:13)—the Lord's words at the time of His flesh-tearing crucifixion remarkably petitioned for favor (pardon unceasing) on those who acted as brute beasts (Ps. 73:22) before Him. *He forgave* (Luke 23:34)!

And to all those who are citizens of His kingdom (Phil. 3:20), those whom He has appointed as heirs of eternal life (Titus 3:7), we operate in His strength, having been vested with His full authority to bestow on anyone else as undeserving as ourselves an abundant pardon reminiscent of that which was meted out to us (Isa. 55:7). We are Blood-bought ambassadors (2 Cor. 5:18–20) whose lives cannot resist telling the mysterious work of His having been made sin on our behalf, that we might be made the righteousness of God in Him (v. 21). We walk void of restraint, unhampered by any reliance on another fellow being. No strain or expenditure, no stinging moment that we might deluge with forgetfulness can hinder us from declaring that "up to seventy times seven" (Matt. 18:22) we choose to esteem our Faithful Ransom, who "became to us wisdom from God, and righteousness and sanctification, and redemption" (1 Cor. 1:30).

May we labor with eager clarity and purifying faith (2 Pet. 3:11, 14; 1 John 3:3) to consistently honor "Christ, who is our life" (Col. 3:4). He has apportioned us as His sanctified plea: that, on God's behalf, we serve as His appeal to the estranged ones that a measureless reconciliation to Himself is His waiting gift!

Reproached, Yet Welcoming

There are several passages in Scripture I loathe to read. It is not that I fail to value the entirety of His Word or to appreciate the just conviction which turns me back from the error of my wrong thinking (Rom. 12:2). Lord willing, I am growing in respect for all of His revealed and preserved message, as that which men of old recorded under the inspiration of the Holy Spirit (2 Pet. 1:20–21) and which is suitably ordained for our learning, reproof, correction, and training in righteousness (2 Tim. 3:16). But there are parts that are conclusively disheartening, even under the most grace-drenched perspective.

Judges 19 has persistently been one such section. Any glance at a yearlong Bible plan always catches my stomach sinking when that portion comprises the "meat" of my day. The inhumanity, carried out in the fullest *antithesis* of our Good Shepherd (John 10:11, 14–15), inevitably stirs in me a visceral response because of how it focuses on the outworking of man's depravity manifested without restraint.

Mark 4:19, as pointed out by one Bible teacher, also elucidates a pivotal axiom.[49] It is not necessarily an overt affair with the world (James 4:4–5) that will render us fruitless in this life; sometimes it is simply that the Word is choked out of us through a "desire for other things" in comparison to our love for Christ.

Matthew 7:23 leaves its whip bite as well: "I never knew you; depart from Me." How somber it is to consider that there are "just a few being saved" (Luke 13:23), and the remainder abide for the duration of this life as self-deceived, until arriving at that moment where—because there had never been any true intimacy in submitting to His yoke (Matt. 11:28–30)—the Potentate of time[50] will be unable to impart what had been presumed from His hand (see Matt. 7:21).

Jeremiah 23:33 has more recently struck me as the most dramatically disquieting—the kind of passage that stirs one up with the hopelessness, the utter ruin of man apart from God's saving hope in Christ. Speaking to the false prophets who have led the people astray, who have reveled in "falsehoods and reckless boasting" (v. 32), Yahweh, the Covenant-Keeping God, declares in the next verse, "I will abandon you." His ultimate rejection: No admittance, ever, into the eternal communion for which we were designed (Gen. 1:27–3:8; John 17:3). A total malfunctioning[51] and the will of the Adversary is brought to complete fruition: that we would be just as estranged and tormented as he is, bound and afflicted without any relief, for the existence of one's immortal soul.

It is haunting. It is righteous that repayment be made in such a way but candidly horrifying—and it is also a poignant check for any soul enduring a temporary wrong that will never "trespass" this lifetime. What tiny boundaries we hold here (Acts 17:26); what limited stay we maintain (Ps. 90:10, 12)! We groan in these tents (2 Cor. 5:4), in "these carbon shells, these fragile, dusty frames; house canvases of souls."[52]

And yet, we lose sight of how frail, how transitory we truly are (James 4:14), frequently acting as though only that which we see, taste, and feel on this sod-covered globe counts for anything. In such a faulty mindset, we presume there must be more to "snatch" from our experience, and thus (in our entitled disposition) resent anything we suppose to "interrupt" our rights.

Yet what is the real intrusion? Is it not that sinfulness, entering the world and spreading through Adam's descendants, sundered every human's relationship with the Prince of life (Acts 3:15)? Would not our spiritual alienation, apart from Calvary's dominating that rupture, be the most lancing interception of what ought to have proceeded?

By no other means than His renewing atonement, where our lives actually become "hidden with Christ in God" (Col. 3:3), can we entertain the possibility of seeing and touching and proclaiming (1 John 1:1–3), of outright *partaking* of, the Word of life Himself (see John 1:1–4; 15:4–5; 1 Cor. 1:9). "For as through the one man's disobedience, the many were made sinners, even so through the obedience of the One the many will be made righteous" (Rom. 5:19).

The question then becomes a rhetorical exercise. If the Lord Himself—as the innocent One (Luke 23:4, 14–15, 22, 41, 47; 1 Pet. 2:22)—knew what it was to be cast out and to endure reproach (Heb. 13:13), to become severed from God's altogether satisfying communion (Ps. 22:1–2; 2 Cor. 5:21) on account of the mortals who were despising Him (Isa. 49:7; 53:3), then how can we not imitate the acceptance and hospitality He demonstrated toward us (see Lev. 19:33–34)? Even amidst the most hideous instances, in which we have become forsaken, ostracized because we identify too closely with Christ's Name upon us (Isa. 66:5), can we sincerely declare that we prefer a soul's being lost for all eternity—a creature's being damned rather than redeemed—because of the suffering brought to bear on our fleeting days?

If we have not truly come to terms with that answer—being settled in our spirit that we who had made ourselves odious (Deut. 25:16; Ps. 7:11) to the King Eternal have received His royal invitation to fellowship with the Son whom *we* rejected (Matt. 27:23; *cf* Col. 2:13–14)—then we are at risk of defecting from the "word of truth, the gospel," which has every reason to be "constantly bearing fruit ... since the day we heard of it and understood the grace of God in truth" (Col. 1:6). Have we cause for despair when our attendance at that honored ceremony comes by the Father's personal request (see Matt. 22:2; Rev. 19:9)—an inheritance irrevocable (1 Pet. 1:4), yet as sorely unmerited by its recipients as the rejection borne by His Son?

In the Margins

Well-meaning loved ones have repeatedly suggested that I have my Bible rebound. (Maybe the 3M adhesive material functioning as the binding leaves a bit to be desired?) Whatever the case, I could never rightly consider getting this beloved Book rebound, simply because of all the notes I would lose in the margins.

Oftentimes I have managed to collect key phrases or outlines from sermons, but in one case, situated right above a chapter in Matthew, is the intrepid confession made by Polycarp, one of the early church martyrs, when a Roman governor adjured him to deny his Redeemer. His words, reverberating so intimately with verse 13, prompted me to record the fuller scope of God's dealings with us in Christ: "For eighty-six years I have served Christ, and He has done me no wrong. How could I blaspheme my King and my Savior?"[53]

"He has done me no wrong": the exact characterization of the generous landowner, and by extension our Heavenly Father, whom Jesus depicts in Matthew 20 when He asserts, "Friend, I am doing you no wrong" (v. 13). No injustice in Him exists (Job 34:12).

To those laborers who had borne the heat of the day, being paid their agreed-upon wages registered as an injustice—not because the amount had not been settled upfront but because those who trailed in after them had not endured the same hardships yet received equal wages. Resenting that others had been "made equal" to them (v. 12) and, more wickedly, aiming to dictate which actions were "lawful" for the owner, these first-hour workers essentially envied that others were made corresponding benefactors of his lavish kindness (v. 15).

How faithlessly we can compare. How frightfully we lay our life beside another's and demand of the Lord, "What about him?" (John 21:21)—and rightly we receive the reprimand: "What is that to you? You follow Me!" (v. 22).

It is especially tempting, when we discern that the Sovereign who wrested us from death (Isa. 28:18) is as passionate about undertaking a parallel kindness for those who wrought our harm, to disdain His thoughtfulness. The stirring of animosity can resound within us, throbbing in short order with an unholy determination about what is "lawful" for the Owner of our souls to do with what is His own (see Matt. 20:15)—whether in His prerogative to lay down His life and take it up again (John 10:11, 17–18) or in His right to extend mercy to the unbelieving, as He justifies each "as a gift by His grace" (Rom. 3:24).

And yet, were we to drink deeply, to truthfully ponder all the facets of His loving-kindness designed to lead us to repentance (Rom. 2:4), perhaps our question would more firmly center not on the care He has shown our fellow sinners but on the hostility He leveled on the *only legitimate Son*. In truth, if anyone could justifiably object that sinners have received exoneration, it would be the rightful Heir, who shared His inheritance freely (Eph. 1:13–14; 1 Pet. 1:4) but was unobligated to do so apart from the constraints of His love (Matt. 26:53; John 10:11–15, 17–18; cf Heb. 2:10–16).

As those who are rebels by nature—who scoffed at our Heavenly Father's authority, sought for earthly ambitions, and thought nothing of the relationship we were abandoning (see Luke 15:12–13)—it becomes unmistakably clear that only by adoption can we be ushered into any familial relationship (Rom. 8:15; Gal. 4:4–7). One pastor, astutely noting the Father's incredulous choice of us, quipped, "Who wouldn't want to create a bunch of *incompetent, non-loving, adulterous, idolatrous, disobedient children* to call their own?"[54]

The concept that our Father elected to save us from ourselves, and that, to the temporary detriment of His Beloved Child, shapes the reality that, when it comes to our being "chosen of God ... and beloved" (Col. 3:12; Jude 1:1b), our fitting response is to recognize how much "not wrong" He has done us. May we be crushed by the weight of His compassion, which can only lay our mouths in the dust (Lam. 3:29) as we marvel at precisely what this Covenant-honoring Lord accomplished in "forgiving us for all that we have done" (Ezek. 16:63).

No Returns[55]

I have only prayed a few dangerous prayers before—the kind of all-out surrender that will cost the flesh everything; the sort of Spirit-aligned, Christ-exalting self-abasement[56] that desires usefulness to the Divine more earnestly than cheapened contentment with the world's fleeting offers.

One such prayer stands out. I asked God to teach me to love maturely. Yet, even as the years have transpired and God has faithfully supplied me opportunity, there has always remained a clouded sense in my mind of mature love's substance—despite the cross's ample explanation. For some reason I have never been able to articulate the essence of its definition—perhaps because I had somehow inserted the unfounded caveat that a selfless giver should unceasingly expect to be recompensed.

The cross stands in stark contrast. Christ condescended to furnish our desperate souls with righteousness beyond our grasp. Setting aside His rightful glory and every pleasure of heaven (2 Cor. 8:9; Phil. 2:5–8), He robed Himself in our weakened, fallen state to minister salvation to our unhealed souls. He acted, fully acknowledging that He would receive nothing of equal value from the beneficiaries of His rescuing efforts. Out of reverent obedience to His Father, the Son unswervingly committed to addressing the neediness of a weary, sin-stained creation, even though our preservation could only be secured through His beaten body.

Barring all contingencies over the responsiveness of the receiver, mature love enacts measures geared only to the edification of another. No thought to personal interest is entertained. Much like Acts 17 underscores, God, "who made the world and all things in it," since He is Lord of heaven and earth, does not need anything, being Himself the Source, giving "to all people life and breath and all things" (v. 24–25). He bases His movement on no awaited "return" from those He has made the objects of His love (Deut. 7:7; Jer. 31:3).

Defining Himself the pure "God of forgiveness" (Ne. 9:17) by extending Himself to a wrathful and indigent lot, He then converts those rescued ones into ministers of that same reconciliation! What a holy privilege! What a masterfully woven calling: that of recipients-turned-representatives! For, as we experience through our Reconciling Sovereign, our lives—now "qualified" by Him to share in the inheritance of the saints (Ccl. 1:12)—are likewise patterned and equipped to imitate His comprehensive self-sacrifice (Eph. 5:1–2), as we come to love better the soul of one who hates us with venom than any coveted lot, ambition, or treasure (Phil. 2:6–8; Heb. 12:2–3).

How foreign, how utterly alarming—that to love maturely encompasses more than willfully involving ourselves in prospering another being. How much further it extends: to single-mindedly chase every avenue, where we—consciously shedding from our keeping all the comforts, rights, and ease we would have named our own—hasten to the prize of another's exclusive upbuilding.

As we run aground so alien a mission, we come to

embrace a dedicated stance to count the neediness of the offender as more pressing than our rights (see Heb. 10:34); to lay down in sacrifice all earthly goods, if the act could be of benefit to another soul (2 Cor. 12:15); to erupt with godly kindness (Col. 3:12–14) and layers of forgiveness in the face of every wrathful move.

We begin to pursue with faithful humility the spirit who has willfully struck out, as he separates himself from good; to accept the fallout of rebellion without exercising faithlessness or hatred; to receive back graciously, without reproach, the one who caused distress (Philemon 1:17–18); to discern the condition of the heart set against us yet to will only life and health and relief (Ps. 81:13–14, 16; Ezek. 18:23, 32; Zeph. 3:17); to behold his evil yet not to withhold ourselves in malice, resentment, or self-righteousness (Heb. 12:15) but rather welcome him (see Col. 4:10).

Contrary as it is to our composition, we endeavor to shoulder that vulnerable posture of being the sole person to will reconciliation intensively (Rom. 12:18) yet still to offer ourselves as refuge and safe haven when the offender, upon returning, only seeks us because he is empty (see Luke 15:17–19); to uphold and defend, even to esteem and revere (Rom. 12:14; 13:7), the one whose hardness of heart has cost us everything—and yet, to give all, without compulsion but freely (see Phil. 1:14); to respectfully submit (Eph. 5:21), bearing upon ourselves the hatefulness of pride (Jer. 13:17), the injury of oppression (Isa. 30:12), the callousness of afflictions undeserved (Ezek. 13:22), yet to concentrate on Christ Jesus, heaven's Payment, as our Lead (1 Pet. 2:21–23).

We value that harrowing portion to delight actively in the transgressor's good (Rom. 10:1), when he himself forfeited the like—(see Acts 13:46); to shower upon the offending one righteous deeds (Rom. 12:20) when all his actions have cursed and extorted and inflicted severe injury; to bear witness of a love that will outlast evil and disease (1 Cor. 13:7–8a), though we be broken to the limit to explain it (Acts 20:24; Phil. 2:17); to stay, with steady eyes on the good to come, and not—simply because of "the greatness of the ransom" (Job 36:18)—to concede in battle a soul needing rescue from filth and fire (Zech. 3:2–4; *cf* Job 33:18).

Our hearts are shaped to cling to what is good and despise the evil (Rom. 12:9)—even if the greatest source of discomfort be from a surprisingly close source (Ps. 41:9); to neither "dress" nor conceal the wounds with superficiality (1 Sam. 24:11–12; 2 Tim. 4:14) and to rescind nothing of our vulnerability; to purpose to know our Messiah in this outcast state (Ps. 69:9); to not count a wrong against us as any but one which He will avenge (Rom. 12:19)—and which He bore to the cross with far more profound awareness (Ps. 22: 11–18; Heb. 13:13). We learn to seek His hand and find His face[57]—His devotion, His love so full that it could bear sinners and their hideous ways—and still not give them up (see Jer. 31:20; Hos. 11:8).

Love born of true selflessness "breathes" the mission: "We know love by this, that He laid down His life for us; and we ought to lay down our lives for the brethren" (1 John 3:16). As our every faculty becomes enmeshed in the only consequence of import, as we operate in the kind of obedience that has become wholly "convinced of the value, benefit, worth, and superiority of what God has planned,"[58] we hedge closer to embodying what John Bunyan declared when he examined a life well-spent: that "we have not lived until we have done something for someone who can never repay us."

Oh, the danger of loving maturely!

"I Will Repay It"[59]

An unforgiving attitude reveals much about our perceptions. In regard to the one who injured us, our reaction may essentially broil with the hardened tirade, "You're not worth the cost I'm having to pay; you haven't the value of what I am having to endure for you." Praise God that, while those pronouncements reflect our nature, that demeanor was not Christ's toward us.

And yet, as we become acquainted with the consequences of someone else's sins—the actions that exceeded our control and irreversibly changed the fabric of our lives—how do we move from academically assenting to our "no exemption" status from sin's influence to personally laying our defensible rights in the hands of our Savior?

Though Scripture is rife with demonstrations of what a forgiving spirit (and its counterpoint; see, notably, Gen. 34; 2 Sam. 13; Jonah 1, 4) produces, one particular personalized letter from the Apostle Paul to a certain "beloved brother and fellow worker," Philemon, elucidates the heartbeat of Christ's forgiveness. In twenty-five verses, the Lord tucks into this tiny epistle the sweeping truth, born of a flesh-and-blood example through a runaway slave, that God's abundant urging is for the wronged party to release the offender of his guilt.[60]

When Onesimus ran away from his master, he not only stole from Philemon's possessions but had also lived up to the antithesis of his name, "useful." Paul's message to this fellow Christian essentially called Philemon to cease dwelling on what was defrauded and what was owed (Philemon 1:18)—though both were legitimate grievances—and to seek an alternate recompense. This prisoner of the Lord was by no means charging his companion in the faith to deny or minimize the evil Onesimus caused, or the good he was indebted to render; Paul squarely reckoned with the validity of the burden placed upon this godly man. Onesimus had incurred damages and had failed in his obligations.

Yet Paul urged Philemon, in the wake of Onesimus' unfitting departure, to redirect his vantage point. He was not insisting that Philemon diminish the weight of the affront. The egregious offense must not be overlooked but must be dealt with on a totally different basis than the human mind would have it play out! There was nothing in Paul's appeal instructing Philemon to simply concede such wrongs.

Paul wrote instead, "But if he has wronged you in any way or owes you anything, charge that to my account. I, Paul, am writing this with my own hand. I will repay it (not to mention to you that you owe to me even your own self as well)" (v. 18–19). With tender regard for the one who had been wounded, Paul prompted Philemon to ascertain the lofty dimensions of sin's intrusion and to confess that he was powerless to "un-do" the dissolved trust, stolen time, or personal betrayal.

Yet the urgent beckoning was to seek repayment outside of the offender. Paul pointed Philemon's spiritual gaze to the Source of our peace with God when he asserted, in effect, as Christ Himself might say to us, "Yes, this man has caused you much harm, but will you trust Me, the Author of your spiritual restoration, to handle perfectly every crime against you?"

Paul's argument was not that Philemon should view these deep transgressions with an air of flippancy, as though he could receive back this treacherous slave with eyes willfully blinded. Rather, in his lovingly brutal candor, Paul emphasized: the transgression stood, but the offender would not be the supplier of rectification. In the short term, Paul challenged Philemon to lord nothing over his returned (and now regenerate!—see v. 11) slave, whose repentance shone in his resuming his rightful service to Philemon (v. 11–12). In the grander scheme, Paul assured his friend that the debt would be satisfactorily redressed.

Bringing near the conviction that approaches our hearts and offended wills when we are slighted, maligned, mistreated, neglected, assaulted, or devastated by another's sin, Paul fundamentally provokes the reader to a firm settlement: *Will we actively entrust our wounds to the One whom we ourselves have wounded with our sins?* Will we lay in the hands of Him who is righteous, all-knowing, and all-wise the distressing and detrimental results of another person's refusal to part with his own ambitions because it would have "cost him too much"—though the outcome may infiltrate our remaining days? Do we fix our eyes on the criminal and his corrupt actions or on the Righteous Judge and His remedy in providing Himself as the rescue from our rightful death sentence (Ezek. 18:4)?

The aged and incarcerated Apostle was not short on spiritual authority, but rather than command Philemon to forsake retaliation, Paul appealed to him on the basis of their Savior's atonement (Philemon 1:8–9). Through the Holy

Spirit's unction, Philemon was called upon to complete the most actively impassioned task a soul can engage in this side of heaven: to release the transgressor from any liability to suffer for his wrong.[61] If we writhe to digest how we are appointed to express His unmerited reconciliation, let us be swift to note that God has not dealt with us as our sins deserved (Ps. 103:10); He has dealt with *Christ* as our sins deserved.

For as much as we may like to delude ourselves into detachment and exonerate our selfish departure from Him (Philemon 1:15) as reneging on an impersonal obligation, our running from our Maker was *highly* personal. The distance we incited, the divorce we instigated, were rejections—not of a set of rules but of our Sovereign Ruler. How much more severely could we have pierced Him with our rebellion than by thrusting our transgressions into the very flesh of Him (Col. 1:22) with whom we wanted nothing to do?

Let us be sober: the One whom we rejected wholesale received to His deepest recesses the scandal of our desertion. Rather than leave us severed, He shouldered Himself the entire responsibility for calming the aggravated assault upon His character and Person. With unwavering determination to restore to fellowship those once useless to Him, He has ministered to us with the heart-consuming, spirit-humbling, pride-dissolving proof that He will not meet us halfway. Instead, He begets in us the eternal life (Philemon 1:10) that leaves us "no longer slaves" but now "beloved" (v. 16), as vagrant souls at last equipped to commune "forever" (v. 15) with the One to whom we owe our very selves (v. 19).

"Do Not Be Grieved"

Three times in Genesis 45, Joseph stated that it was not human sin but divine election that "sent" him to Egypt (v. 5, 7, 8). And while his brothers, still reeling from the dawning shock that their brother was not dead, absorbed his words, Joseph emphasized the sovereign purpose for life—even for the lives of the ones who had sentenced the innocent. "Now do not be grieved or angry with yourselves, because you sold me here, for God sent me before you to preserve life" (Gen. 45:5).

Joseph's reassurances were meant not only to temper the clinging regret of family members who had never entirely processed their treachery and deceit (see Gen. 42:21–22) but also to acknowledge with worship-filled certainty that God had a fuller purpose that He was orchestrating on behalf of all involved. As Job would word it, "Who among all these does not know that the hand of the LORD has done this, in whose hand is the life of every living thing, and the breath of all mankind?" (12:9–10).

And it was because he would not retreat from that larger perspective that this displaced Hebrew could entreat his siblings to not live in self-condemnation: "Do not be grieved or angry with yourselves" (Gen. 45:5). His words ring with the sound of Job's consoling aims: "I could strengthen you with my mouth, and the solace of my lips could lessen your pain" (16:5). His greatest concern was not centered on vengeance, but on assuaging his brothers' sorrow from becoming "excessive," on meting out protective measures of forgiveness and comfort (see 2 Cor. 2:7). In short, he exhorted his brothers to partake of the mercy being extended to them.

What must that have sounded like to his brothers' ears? For this veritable ruler of Egypt, treated as subhuman by his scheming brothers who would have all but extinguished his life, was saying to these men that all of their transgressions—their willful jealousies, their murder plot and treatment of him as chattel, even their corrupt fabrication as, for multiple years, they maintained an infrastructure of deceit before their father—were not only forgiven but were also implemented as tools by which God brought about Joseph's movement into a strategic place: the point at which God could wield him as a vessel of divine deliverance.

The Sovereign One's purpose transcended the brothers' cruel intentions. Even before they had gnashed at their favored sibling for evil, God ordained that His servant, Joseph, be positioned as deliverer for a people whose need amidst famine would yet arise. Included in that providential care were the very siblings who sought Joseph's destruction.

And so, in that moment, the shamed brothers were forced to grapple with the fact that God—who had witnessed their persecution of an innocent man, and who had all those years left His hand heavy upon them (Ps. 32:3–4) as they strove to conceal their blood-guilt—was the same One earnestly desirous of their preservation!

What must it have been to receive that wincing, good news; to discover that from the recipient of their harshest treatment effused a reverent boldness, melting into praise, as Joseph overflowed with undaunted gratitude? His words nearly tremble in gracious summation: *"Yes, I was damaged, but you were spared."*

With brushstrokes alluding to what Paul would later write in Romans, the condemnation under which the traitorous men lived was completely dispelled (Rom. 8:1); there was no way to reckon to them as unrighteousness what God scoured from the ledgers. Joseph would not requite them by his own hand, would not "do to them as they had done to him" (Prov. 24:29).

Yet amazingly, the merciful restraint of justice was only heightened by Joseph's deliberately dismantling his brothers' remorse with an untainted benediction! Releasing his siblings of their indebtedness, he further obliged himself to be their provision during the remainder of the famine (Gen. 45:11), to secure for them the best of all the land of Egypt (Gen. 45:18, 20), and to exhibit a humble mercy that would not demand recompense for their unfair dealings (see Gen. 50:17, 19, 21).

His abounding pardon reflects the quality of Christ's love, depicted by Puritan John Flavel in his composition "The Father's Bargain with the Son"—a brief meditation depicting the tender arrangement for redemption coordinated among the members of the Trinity. With the Father's indictment that His creatures had "utterly undone themselves" and exposed themselves to His justice, His Son allowed the full weight of mankind's depravity, and its rightful punishment, to fall upon the second Person of the Godhead with His voluntary response,

> O My Father, such is My love to, and pity for them, that rather than they shall perish eternally, I will be responsible for them as their Surety ... I will rather choose to suffer Thy wrath than they should suffer it: upon Me, My Father, upon Me be all their debt.

As those preserved alive by the One we had sold out; as creatures now made "sons of God through faith in Christ Jesus" (Gal. 3:26), we commune with the One who was "content to undertake" for us the agonizing obedience that summoned to His Being God's uncensored wrath (Isa. 53:10). As we enter into the "fellowship of His sufferings" (Phil. 3:10), our lives, patterned after His, bear up patiently under sorrow for the sake of conscience toward God (1 Pet. 2:19–20)—because the One living and laboring through us embraced to Himself the very undoing from which our healing arose (Isa. 53:5; 1 Pet. 2:24).

Incapacitated

For some people the appeal of heaven comes in the sheer negation of the curse—the removal of tears, the fact that mourning cannot enter in and corrupt what is made beautiful and pristine and entirely new (Rev. 21:4–5). The way it was made to be, the way it is heading to be—the way it isn't nearly yet.

I cannot say I have been entirely divorced from that sentiment. Oftentimes, the wonder of seeing God face to face is so utterly severed from my reasoning that I can barely muster more than a paltry appreciation. Still, the concept that enraptures me most profoundly is the truth that, as one who will be glorified, sabotaged no more by the fabric of my own being (1 Pet. 2:11), I will no longer contain any ability to hurt my Savior! Sinning will be incapacitated!

After all of the times iniquities have cropped up from the hollows of this chest (Matt. 15:19) and bled out the truth of my identity—not that I "sometimes sin" but that I am a sinner (Rom. 5:8) by nature (Ps. 51:5)—the need to be forgiven will finally be expunged (or so I tend to reason).

In reality, our offense against an infinite God would take all of eternity to repay, as hell itself affirms (Matt. 25:41, 46; 2 Thess. 1:9), and so Christ's pardon is an atonement that *covers* us for all eternity from the rightful wrath we had been accumulating for ourselves (see Rom. 2:5). However, the notion that all hostility and malice and agitation, all selfish striving and vain ambition and untempered jealousy, will suddenly be slain leaves me ... awed. To be able to function aright, to honestly pour upon the all-deserving One (Rev. 4:11; 5:9, 12) the reverent and dignifying honor, the zealous, adoring submission He fully owns—"Indeed it is His due!" (Jer. 10:7)—causes great rejoicing to well up. We will behold this One whom we have long awaited and, as we are incited to do even now, will "greatly rejoice with joy inexpressible and full of glory" (1 Pet. 1:8).

In the meanwhile, there is the gritty service of aligning ourselves with the beings we will one day become: of moving with repentance toward Him and embracing the rest that comes from agreeing with His evaluation of our wrongs, of entering into the quietness that breathes inside our extended trust (Isa. 30:15) in the character of our Lord. And there is the complementing action of liberating fellow offenders from their wrongs against us—all records turned to cinders (see 1 Cor. 13:5), and a full desire to pour unmitigated blessing upon the heads (Rom. 12:20–21) of those who are not earning any "honorable" status in our sight.

For *we* were sinners (Rom. 5:8). *We* were enemies (v. 10). We practiced and constituted the very abominations God explicitly hates (see Deut. 25:16). And yet He caused "righteousness and peace" to kiss each other (Ps. 85:10), pulling into communion the blamelessness of His Son and the reconciliation with His holy standard that we fiercely lacked.

Our role is not to shirk the identity lavished upon us but to abide intentionally within the "brand-marks" (Gal. 6:17) implicit in communicating His extravagant love. Although we are now exempted from the spiritual death (Rev. 20:6) we had labored fastidiously to "earn," we continue to sojourn alongside others as sorely tainted by the Fall. The interplay will not find us unscathed.

Though we will one day be incapable of inflicting further harm on Christ or on His creatures, we are called for the interim to bear the devastation and destruction that underscore sin's lethal ramifications. Our time between now and our arrival to our eternal home, where we enjoy His measureless presence, will prove us marred from the warfare. In fact, it is only fitting.

For the God who resolved to spare us His wrath also deigned to wear for all eternity the traces of what our sin inflicted upon His soul: the wounds of His being slain (Rev. 5:6), which will forever serve as the incorruptible reminder of every believer's "entry fee"[62] into our heavenly abode. In recognition of our costliness to Him, we need not recoil at the injuries we sustain, for "we never leave the battlefield without scars—but they are only our family resemblance to our Eternal Savior."[63]

The Litmus Test

The solitary answer to our degenerate condition comes through the Father's ending the catastrophe of war we had waged against Him. As the Apostle John writes, "We have an Advocate with the Father, Jesus Christ the righteous" (1 John 2:1). Humanity's hope arises from no other mediation (1 Sam. 2:25; 1 Tim. 2:5).

The sheer fact that the One who *defines* holiness became undiluted sin Himself (2 Cor. 5:21) confronts us with our two-fold incompetence: both in our delinquency to carry out the one righteous command we were to have performed (Gen. 2:17) and then in our inadequacy to remedy the relationship shorn to pieces by our self-elevation (Isa. 64:6–7). Adequately termed the "morally insane,"[64] we stand with vain delusions entirely if we muse we can repair the gargantuan chasm between Blamelessness Himself and our guilt-ridden state.

Christ alone is our Arbitrator. Apart from Him, we are either eternally at rest—or forever severed from His grace, estranged from the hope of His approbation. There is no middle ground. God has always only accepted one Life as meeting standard. Though we are ensnared by the deceptions that leave us recalcitrant instead of repentant, He is not surprised (as we are; Jer. 17:9) by our depravity.

Interposing with a Champion (Isa. 19:20), He designed that our legal clearance come because of His activity and for His acclaim. If we are justified, it is by His kindness; if we are alienated, it is because of our hard-heartedness (Rom. 2:5).

Nineteenth-century theologian Charles Bridges expounds on this concept of our intending to "own" any of the righteous accounting we have been granted in Christ:

> When the sinner is held back from the gospel by a sense of unworthiness, his worthiness is the implied ground of his coming to the gospel—his work—not Christ's. When the Christian longs for a deeper view of sin, and love to Christ, and forgets, that, when attained, he will have the same need as before of the blood and righteousness of Christ—this is again to put spiritual self in place of Christ. ... If our ground be sure in Christ, let this be our only confidence in our highest frame; and it will be a satisfactory stay in our lowest.

We have no place within ourselves to which we can attribute this restoration. We are His by His doing, "and that not of ourselves" (Eph. 2:8). God Himself provided the sacrifice (Gen. 22:8); He has "given it to us on the altar to make atonement for our souls" (Lev. 17:11).

Luke 7 paints a fairly vivid portrait of God's handiwork. Invited to the home of a Pharisee, Jesus pointed out the nature of love expressed by a woman who had been forgiven of many sins. In verse 47, He explained the reason for her extravagant display: "Therefore, I tell you, her many sins have been forgiven—as her great love has shown. But whoever has been forgiven little loves little" (NIV).

The litmus test then comes. To what degree are we cleaving to the truth that He is the security of our approval? How are we valuing the unearned favor accorded us? If we are rightly esteeming His unwarranted compassion, our actions will communicate love without limit to those who have committed wrongs against us; however, if others' sins loom large in our estimation, we have almost certainly afforded His mercy a diminished appraisal from the treasured status we once knew it to hold.

Although we may declare our willingness to forgive (to voluntarily absorb the costs another has incurred) and to refrain from vengeance; and although we may even come to terms with our inherent guilt in the greatest crime of all humanity (see Acts 2:23), we may be errant in our thinking if persuaded that we have exonerated the offending party while still holding rigid parameters on re-entry.

Though there are certainly instances where it is both unsafe and unwise to allow a person continued access at times when damage or injury are accompanied by no repentant action, it is otherwise wrong of us if we presume that pardon is a cold, calculated, impersonal manifestation of a superior will that has opted mechanically to accept another's fault without a grudge. Christ does not receive us that way.

By contrast, He avails Himself to us with extreme tenderheartedness, warmly poured out. He ushers us back into "the level of intimacy appropriate to the relationship" before any sever occurred. While we will never outgrow our need for continual cleansing from our sin (1 John 1:9), believers in God's Son have risked all to trust that His atoning work will not leave us bereft of hope when we close our eyes on this world. We anticipate the "real-er" communion, pledged by our Lord and sealed by His Spirit, in the eternal home awaiting us. Though we cannot accurately fathom the meaning of that entry, undivided communion with God the Father and with His Son (Rev. 21:3; 22:4) is sufficient evidence that the God of grace extends insurmountable privileges to those who ordered the nailing of His Son to a piece of wood.

So where are there holdouts lurking within us, demanding with premeditated *in*hospitality that certain prerequisites be satisfied? Are we barricading ourselves with formalities? Are we masking either self-protective or self-righteous motives with an overlay of "standards" that must be fulfilled before we again grant permission for another clay-garbed, fallen human being to draw near?

What hurdle did God pose for *us* that we should have to prove ourselves "worthy" before returning to Him? Do we not remember how, in Jesus's parable of the exquisitely loving father, the man who had been disgraced by his son bolted from a lengthy distance to greet his estranged child (Luke 15:20)? How he *silenced* the measured terms his weary offspring felt obliged to place upon his own homecoming (v. 19, 21–24)? How he overrode his loved one's subpar attempts at a "remedy" denying any but the closest reunification?

Although our efforts at reconciliation cannot mirror in full the resplendent love of our Gracious Father, yet His compassion pulses within us. We will certainly struggle (most every day that we reside "tented" in this flesh; 2 Cor. 5:1) to relinquish our alleged rights and regard foremost the wellbeing of the one who deeply wounded us, but such endeavors will prompt us to stay inevitably riveted upon the cross—which should have been labeled with our name.

Restored to fellowship with the faithful God, who fitted us for fellowship through His Son and our Savior (1 Cor. 1:9), we will—however feebly at first—be shaped to a love of right values, as we esteem the "unforsaken-ness" He has afforded to our ravaged souls. By the Spirit of God, who "gives life to the dead and calls into being that which does not exist" (Rom. 4:17), we may even delightedly discover that He wells within us an outflow of the same comforting mercy He caused us to receive (see 2 Cor. 1:3–4).

May we love much because *He* has!

Our Boast

Tomorrow marks what would have been the sixty-eighth anniversary of my grandparents. By God's grace, they reached forty years, which—considering the toll Nana's earlier stroke had taken upon her body—called for our immediate family's cross-country trip in honor of the celebration. When my grandparents were graced with a joyous *sixtieth* anniversary, our family was awed and humbled by the extended years the Lord bestowed, not only for the continuance of their relationship but also for our grandmother's godly heritage, whose echoes have been felt throughout this family.

It was in the final hours of my grandmother's earthly stint, according to a scene recounted by a loved one, that the Christ-like nature of this one, short in stature and yet towering in generous love, plainly shone. Apparently, when one of her daughters commented on the coolness of the air-conditioned hospital, this consummate mother, ever providing for her children, took it upon herself to peel off the blanket covering her declining frame and ensure that her daughter received its warmth.

John 19 often recalls to me her action—because of the utter mindfulness of another's need in the midst of one's most dire straits. With a cowardly governor (v. 6, 8, 12–13,

19, 22) defaulting to fear of man instead of reaching an honorable decision; with self-absorbed soldiers gambling for this alleged criminal's last tangible belongings just beneath His place of execution (v. 23–24); and with tongues wagging their mocking insults at an hour when God had forsaken His soul (Ps. 22:1–2), as "a worm and not a man" (v. 6); this Christ peered down amidst His labored breaths to behold the woman whose own adherence to Yahweh's plan (to carry the Son of the Most High in her unwed body) could have resulted in a death sentence, had the man to whom she was engaged not been "a righteous man" who treated her mercifully (see Matt. 1:19). The Beloved disciple records,

> When Jesus then saw His mother, and the disciple whom He loved standing nearby, He said to His mother, "Woman, behold, your son!" Then He said to the disciple, "Behold, your mother!" From that hour the disciple took her into his own household. (John 19:26–27)

The Lamb, *in that moment* being slain, this One who had lived all His earthly span for the completion of this desolate hour, in which all the forces of evil appeared to triumph over the Deviser of life (Gen. 2:7), took note. Although His unparalleled turmoil and excruciating torture might have distracted Him from viewing the "sword piercing the heart" (Luke 2:35) of His loved one, although His own unspeakable rawness might have clutched at His attention with shrieking grittiness, yet He all His compassions were kindled and His heart was turned over within Him (Hos. 11:8).

That is the sweep of the cross. It is the logic-defying

truth that this Holy God, who plunged Himself into the havoc of our sullied mission to divorce ourselves from Him, occupied Himself with a reclamation of those under self-inflicted devastation—although the endeavor required Him to grab hold of more heinous repercussions than the rescued ones would ever endure.

We were preserved; He was punished. We were spared; He was shattered. We were held back from the slaughter to which we were headed; He was the innocent Offering who stole our sentence.

He came; He inserted Himself where He had no right to belong—in the mockery of a traitor's kiss and in the perverted sham of a trial, in a criminal's place of hanging and in the crosshairs of holy wrath's vengeance for the wickedness we could never expunge.

It is, as Martin Luther expresses, "the most damnable and pernicious heresy that has ever plagued the mind of man" to believe that "somehow he could make himself good enough to deserve to live with an all-holy God." But it is also the matchless grace of our Lord Jesus Christ to have divulged to us the saving knowledge of sin's purification, revealed through the tender mercy with which God visited His people (Luke 1:77–78).

How can we not, how dare we not—find Him to be our exclusive boast? As even His earthly mother proclaimed of the One who would render her soul righteous through His deliverance, "My soul exalts the Lord, and my spirit has rejoiced in God my Savior" (Luke 1:46–47).

Showing Mercy

Be kind to one another, tender-hearted, forgiving each other, just as God in Christ also has forgiven you.

—Ephesians 4:32

"Not Overwhelmed"

As finite creatures, our strong tendency is to construe God's answers as errors. Perhaps it disturbs us that the Lord, whose slowness to anger (Ne. 9:17) invariably eclipses our own (James 1:19), deals more tenderly with His offenders than we do with those who have violated us. Is it some haunting, lyrical strain to envision that "treasured guest" (see Luke 15:24, 32) becomes the stamp firmly placed on men and women God counts as "welcomed vagabonds" and "remedied defectors"? Does it nourish our self-justified ruling of "indecency" to consider that the unseemly ones are the sort the Lord receives back with gusto?

Aaron typifies the conundrum. Exodus 28 would be nowhere near as exasperating were it not a decree issued directly from the Omniscient One who—needing none to testify about what resides in the heart of man (John 2:24–25; cf Gen. 6:5)—was imparting to Moses strict instruction on how this soon-to-be spiritual representative for the nation would be garbed. The fact that Aaron's younger brother could be gathering meticulous notes on the fine twisted linen (v. 8) and the gold filigree settings (v. 13), while Aaron was at the foot of the mountain, readying to lead the recently freed slaves into a bondage more palpable than any visited on them by their Egyptian taskmasters (Exod. 32:7–8), creates havoc enough.

Exodus 40 smacks of a seemingly worse affront. While Aaron rightly bore the blame (Exod. 32:21, 35) for the congregation's mass fall into egregious idolatry—as it is entirely fitting for the leader of God's people to be held to a higher accountability (James 3:1; *cf* Jer. 25:34–35; Ezek. 34:1–10; Luke 11:40–52)—his being chosen by the Lord to stand as minister before Him incurred no alteration. The Faithful One, who had foresworn the honor over him in chapter 28, made good on His word in ordination proceedings just twelve chapters later.

Now that is *not* to say that God winked at Aaron's sin. With an eye ever to the mount of Crucifixion—in which He "justifies the ungodly" (Rom. 4:5) by marking the godly One *un*justified in exchange (see Rom. 3:21–26)—He has administered justice for every iniquity and transgression committed across the ages for those He would deem righteous. Indeed, "If the LORD should mark iniquities … who could stand?" (Ps. 130:3). No compromise in His holy judgment exists (see Rom. 3:25–26).

But at the same time, it can pose a stumbling block to absorb that God, whose "mercies are over all His works" (Ps. 145:9), appears far more restrained in His hostilities than we might be. Why is it that the One who surveys every fiber of creation comprehensively, objectively, and flawlessly; and who "searches all hearts, and understands every intent of the thoughts" (1 Chron. 28:9), can receive so freely those who have raised their fists against Him with utter vehemence?

And why, in turn, are we content to let the offender make the arduous journey back to us—on our own terms—as we watch those who damaged our trust or dignity be forced to grovel for our hand of mercy? Does it so indulge our prideful exploits?

If it is infuriating enough to witness how defilement on Aaron's part derailed nothing of the divine intent, is the anger potentially because we fail to see our own lewdness? Are we shortsighted about the purification we have been handed (2 Pet. 1:9), which attends us through no "fault" of our own?

Or, if it is not necessarily the soft-heartedness of the Father that dredges up our "out of joint" assessments, is there some other covert temperament, born of an innate sense of what is "fair," to presuppose that any re-entry is out of the question? What is it in our hearts—bound up so closely with the scandal we have observed—that intentionally guards all points of access with unabated vigor? Have we so successfully blinded ourselves to the wretchedly incorrigible and woefully inadequate souls we *are*—whom Christ has nonetheless ushered into uninhibited communion through His torn flesh (Heb. 10:20)?

Perhaps at the core of our warding off the reinstatement of another, we are deeming *ourselves* "unworthy of eternal life" (Acts 13:46). Perhaps, as we gauge our acceptance with the wrong measuring stick, we are clasping to ourselves the notion that—just as it is completely unfitting for the King of Creation to receive *us* under His kind auspices—so every other defiant creature must also languish under remorse brought to its bitter fruition.

In a similar situation, the church in Corinth received from the Apostle Paul letters exhorting the members to take seriously both the matter of chastening one of their own (when they had been arrogantly condoning his immorality;

1 Cor. 5:1–6), and then of comforting him (when he had been crushed by the weightiness of genuine repentance). As a vested shepherd, who powerfully loved the flock he had pastored (see 2 Cor. 2:1–5), Paul tempered the church's extremes, whereby the Body had left an unrepentant man in the peril of unchecked sin, and then—when he had turned—had left him nearly comfortless with the censure. In chapter 2 of Paul's second letter, we read, "Sufficient for such a one is this punishment which was inflicted by the majority" (v. 6).

By all means, the church had done well in "turning a sinner from the error of his way" and so "saving his soul from death" (James 5:20). The objective now was in staving off the disconsolate state of this man who, once vaunting his sins, was near to becoming inundated in the process of forsaking his former baseness. Paul fleshes out the reasons for a cessation of harsh consequences: "So that on the contrary you should rather forgive and comfort him, otherwise such a one might be overwhelmed by excessive sorrow" (2 Cor. 2:7).

To dig into the word a little further, "comfort" comes from Latin's *con fortis*—with strength. The role of the believers surrounding this contrite soul was to infuse him with the inner fortitude to face his sins head-on while simultaneously tasting the relief of a pardon that scoured his soul of any impropriety. The work of Christ's Body is the work Christ Himself undertook: that—just as God has not dealt with us according to our sins (Ps. 103:10)—we have no right to degrade a fellow Image-bearer. Stretching back from the *Pentateuch,* God's principle of maintaining a reprimanded soul's dignity stands fast (see Deut. 25:3).

Yet Paul, inspired by the ultimate Forgiver, intensifies his command with one further step of compassion: "Wherefore

I urge you to reaffirm your love for him" (2 Cor. 2:8). A mere covering of the transgressions is not adequate. While nothing apart from the Son's setting him free (John 8:36) is necessary for a man's total cleansing, still it behooves the believers around him to use no restraint: to unleash on him the shocking reassurance that—even when his uncontrolled "self" was raging at its worst—he could never have outrun the benediction chasing him down (see Deut. 28:2; Ps. 23:6).

For have we not—through our "Apostle and High Priest," who caused us to become "partakers of a heavenly calling" (Heb. 3:1)—been halted in our self-loathing as divine grace has afforded us the opportunity to lash out at our worst and still find ourselves met with a steadfast, insistent blessing? Have we any prerogative to withhold from another the grace He has manifested toward us?

Our purpose for remaining on this globe has everything to do with nothing we have earned! We are now freed—not just to offer an impersonal affirmation of legal cleansing that "all has been forgiven," but far more personally, the tenderhearted, impassioned cry that we "welcome home" the one who has waywardly departed from the truth. Imparting to a fellow soul the gospel's grace comes with the infusion of bestowing our very lives (1 Thess. 2:8). It is not enough to dismiss the debt on cold and calculated terms when we have the full throttle joy of being able to declare, with impelling good will, that we bow our knees before the Father,

> that He would grant you, according to the riches of His glory, to be strengthened with power through His Spirit in the inner man, so

that Christ may dwell in your hearts through faith; and that you, being rooted and grounded in love, may be able to comprehend with all the saints what is the breadth and length and height and depth, and to know the love of Christ which surpasses knowledge, that you may be filled up to all the fullness of God. (Eph. 3:14–19)

An Invitation

Still in my keeping is a bulletin from at least a decade ago, which was intended—with its blank side on the back—to serve as the ideal spot for sermon notes. Apparently my scribbling hand caught the attention of a fellow parishioner—one who also tended to sit toward the back of the sanctuary and whose fascination questioned what during the service had precipitated such fierce writing. Little had he known that my heart was racing with one refrain, which tempered the shockwaves of the turmoil I could scarcely subdue. In a lilting exercise, the only scribing my pen could tolerate were the words, numerous times over down the page: "You are faithful." No other hope sufficed (Ps. 71:5).

For one who felt thrust into a situation I had not welcomed, I found myself awash in the cognizance that every mental reception of my Father's stalwart promises—that He would accomplish what concerns me (Ps. 138:8), that He could not lie (Nu. 23:19), that He had led me in right paths (Prov. 4:11)—grounded me with an ever-increasing certainty that He was my steadiness even when all other footing crumbled.

The tension centered, in the tedium, not on the "prayer that kept returning to my bosom" (Ps. 35:13) but on the unenthusiastic rawness of being a "patient when wronged" bondservant (2 Tim. 2:24). To be subjected to the stewardship of one who might wield it improperly edged me frequently into the plea that His defense arc above the chaos.

Yet I stalled out with perplexity over how Christ could *willfully* embrace such subjection. While "submission" was in His vocabulary, "helplessness" never was. He enacted each measure of rescue with concerted effort to perfect the plan laid out from eternity past. From squirming babe to mangled corpse, He placed His Person in the keeping of those who would acclaim Him at birth (Luke 2:25–32) and entomb Him at death (Mk. 15:46). Nothing shied away from the "no recourse" gateway in His partaking of our flesh that He might empty us of fear (Heb. 2:14–15).

I, on the other hand, felt caught up in a whirlwind of unrelenting circumstances that changed beyond my foreseeing, undercut me beyond my expectation, and "complicated" beyond my approval. If anything could be matched with my Savior's demeanor, I knew it not. He *shouldered* vulnerability of His own blessed will; I was doing well to *survive* it.

Yet if this Self-Existent, All-Knowing, Unchanging, Faultless, and Spotless God could ready Himself to near the hate-filled, insurgent delegation who chased after Him with venom (Luke 19:14) and not dismantle such fury with coercive strong-arming but His own self-abasement, then there had to be some manner of "being" in which I could follow suit. He had, after all, left a profitable example (1 Pet. 2:21).

His contentment had not been found in the visible hands that would wrap around Him, but in the everlasting arms undergirding Him (Deut. 33:27). He lived and died to please the God who enlisted Him (2 Tim. 2:4) in the powerful work of overthrowing sin's lethal forces. His deliberate roles—in forsaking His royal privileges (Phil. 2:6–7) and in baring His Soul to a rejecting people (Ps. 14:2–3; Isa. 65:1)—constituted a "yielding" directed entirely upward. This Missionary, sent to proclaim truth without hesitancy, kept at the fore that His work always entailed completing the will of the One who laid the charge upon Him (John 4:34; 5:30; 6:38). Submitting brought exaltation vertically (Matt. 26:39, 42, 44). Even in His final act of bowing His head before giving up His Spirit (John 19:30), He divulged His singular Audience.[65] The relationship with His Father drove every action.

And so it became in my case. Although my vision could behold little more than the "fringes of His ways" (Job 26:14), it was through the plunging intervals of heightened trust and snagging discouragement that the Lord kept shaping me to the veracity of His eternal Word's being my lifeline. Made to dwell with Him in the final outcome, I was being presented vast opportunities amidst the "testing ground" to forge ahead into what that new relationship with Him will be, when nothing unfastens my eyes from the truth that He alone is my Ambition and the Object of all my affections.

While the reticence in my spirit paralleled nothing of my Saving Shepherd's voluntary availability, at least at the onset of the ordeal, His Spirit began imparting to me the confided knowledge (Ps. 25:14) that, by stepping into that oppositional scenario, I had entered a sacred space where God could grant "repentance leading to the knowledge of the truth" for the person trapped in the devil's snare (2 Tim. 2:25–26). Accepting the seizure of what was mine enabled a showing of sympathy (Heb. 10:34) to him who had imprisoned himself by spurning the Most High (Ps. 107:10–11). With no ability in myself to deliver another (Ps. 49:7–8), still God chose my being subjugated in weakness as the instrument by which He engaged the disquieted spirit of another.

In the process of my esteeming more highly that awkward post (of dying to my own aspirations as I was "handled," as it were, in whatever fashion the Lord had purposed), I came to appreciate that seeking affirmation apart from our ultimate Authority (Rom. 14:4, 10, 12; 2 Cor. 5:9–10), is—as a beloved friend enjoys the phrase—the "height of lunacy."

If my tears, counseled by His strategic placement of me, meant the liberation of one soul held captive; if my exposure to the counterpoints of all that seemed decent and natural and sane meant the exercise of His good pleasure (Phil. 2:13) within me, then my rejoinder surmounted the irreverent circumstances and the mind-boggling readjustments that bore into the cavity of my chest. I could "suffer these things" without shame, well knowing the One whom I had believed (2 Tim. 1:12).

Tempting as it is to characterize forgiveness as a transaction with the offender; enticing as it is to consume ourselves with the hope of personal acknowledgement from the source of soreness that implodes our existence, if we settle for the truncated hope of being noticed in our writhing by the one responsible, we taint our Christ-bearing Image. For our Intervening Deity afforded room for, and even winsomely invited to Himself, the inexorable pangs of being placed into the hands of godless men (Acts 2:23). As resident aliens in this world (Heb. 11:9; 1 Pet. 1:1; 2:11) but citizens of His kingdom (John 18:36–37), we are apportioned to fulfill the yearning of the Trinity: to mirror Christ's humility of service, in which the sacrificial depletion that enriched us (2 Cor. 8:9) stemmed from Jesus's obedience to the plan birthed in His Father's delight (Isa. 53:10; Col. 1:19–20).

Sweetness

If reconciliation is the condition of being brought into favor after a natural estrangement,[66] then God, who is the Deviser of such a contented state, is an Almighty Healer and Gracious Friend all at once! He imparts to His own creatures, those infused with His spiritual life (Ezek. 36:25–27; Rom. 4:17; 2 Cor. 5:17; Gal. 6:15), the surpassing joy of being messengers of His Beloved Son, in whom true restoration was completed (see Col. 2:13–14). In His kindest move (Rom. 2:4), He tucked us into His life (Col. 3:3) and now pours out the streaming flow of grace's incarnation through the remnant He has left upon this earth. As believers in the Beloved (Eph. 1:4–6; Jude 1:1b), we steward the splendid and royal role of being a living reassurance to those who surround us of just how cleansing our Messiah's blood truly is.

For too many Christians, the propensity is to plod on under a malaise of uncertainty that His atoning work was conclusive. While our flesh, tearing at every good intention, reminds us that we are both hopeless and helpless to fight the enemy within (see 1 Pet. 2:11), we can sound forth the exuberant praise that even the travesties within us validate our never-to-be-outlived dependence on our Precious Savior!

And that is where the delight of *supplying* forgiveness

steps in! For, just as our daily confession sets low our pride in imagining we can somehow bolster self-effort, opportunities in which we have the prerogative to extend forgiveness allow our hearts to reinforce for the one who may be languishing that, compelled by the love of Christ (2 Cor. 5:14–15), we are willfully inclined to "consume with favor" those who have done us harm. Intense exhilaration springs from the autonomy that resists awaiting another's repentance and proactively commits to the temporal and eternal wellbeing of a fellow creature.

For over six years, I had been enshrouded in the daily practice of choosing to forgive another human being. The act was perfunctory at times but always attended with the pleasant relief that embarking on the holy enterprise honored the Lord. While I may not have entered more than the intellectual echelon of acclaiming the worth of pardon, I had at least freed from my keeping any bitterness that gnawed incessantly.

It was not until my being exposed to Jonathan Edwards' "Resolutions"[67] that God tore into me with a far more distinctive manner of thinking. For this revivalist preacher, who endeavored to live wholly sold-out for his God, the profit in articulating his life's purpose engendered him to record a list that he could revisit frequently, as a personalized check on his heavenward direction. Under the sure admission that no labor could be conducted without divine aid, he wrote, among others, the following statements:

> 7. Resolved, never to do anything, which I should be afraid to do, if it were the last hour of my life.

> 9. Resolved, to think much on all occasions of my own dying, and of the common circumstances which attend death.
>
> 25. Resolved, to examine carefully, and constantly, what that one thing in me is, which causes me in the least to doubt of the love of God; and to direct all my forces against it.
>
> 56. Resolved, never to give over, nor in the least to slacken my fight with my corruptions, however unsuccessful I may be.

In this humble minister's intentionality, God bade me kill passivity. It was not only insufficient to strip myself of malice; it was not the full representation of Christ. If tenderheartedness could not surface in me—because there was none beneath the heavy shrouds of resentment I had to keep unpeeling—then my volition was cruising well below altitude. Even if none of the words resembled my gut, even if contriving a benediction felt as strange on my tongue as the first words uttered in a foreign language, I had to expound to my soul, as the psalmist taught *his* (see Ps. 42:5, 11), that "wisdom is vindicated by her deeds" (Matt. 11:19); that out of reverence for God, my heart sought to elevate the care of another soul, though I contended that my spirit had been disregarded.

By His Spirit's guidance, the list flowed quickly, with the foundational line being *"Resolved, by Your grace,"*

> to recognize that the rewards of obedience will far outstrip any of the sacrifice by "a hundredfold"

to determine to give preference, and to submit my spirit, in holy reverence for You.

to good, and not harm; to will blessing, edification, eternal wellbeing.

to make manifest the nature of Your forgiveness, by holding no record of wrong, but harboring a heart of tenderness, even as You in Christ have forgiven me.

to deliver the message of Your salvation, of unrepentant, unconditional love, which makes itself known in its generosity and selflessness; and to abdicate any position which would cause estrangement, resentment, jealousy, or unrest.

to believe that You … are ever about Your work, and are fully gracious in allowing me participation (in this labor).

to treat this one with the dignity of a person made in Your image.

notwithstanding conflicts or misunderstandings, to seek healthy and courteous ways to listen, and to interact with patience and insight, humility and foresight.

God, grant me grace to carry out what You have desired. … Amen.

The forgiver has available much leeway to articulate the nature of our Forgiving Lord. While the result may never include the recipient's awakening to grace, to the believer, such a presentation focuses our cognizance on all we have been forgiven, and creates a fuller-orbed contrition for the wrongs we have yet to confess as we humbly depend upon the love binding us (Hos. 11:4).

For, when we understand that we are called to advance the wellbeing of others (see Eph. 4:15–16; Col. 1:25), we begin to shoulder our God-ordained role. Bowing ourselves down gladdens us, because we are severely assured that our greatest employ is not in being personally edified (Rom. 15:2–3; 1 Cor. 10:24) but passionately expended (2 Cor. 12:15).

And as we gratefully receive that sweetness of purpose, we become increasingly satisfied in our immanent Savior, who petitioned His Father when He was little more than a footfall from the death He had prepared before time (Rev. 13:8). With mighty "wrestlings" and resolutions on our behalf, long before we came into existence (John 17:20) or understood our crimes, Jesus beseeched His Father for the sake of those coated with the blood-guilt of provoking His tribulation—that we would experience joy (John 17:13), protection from the evil one (v. 15), sanctification in the truth (v. 17), commissioning as His messengers (v. 18), unity in Him and with fellow believers (v. 21, 23), and the designation as those whom He loves and who will behold His glory (v. 23).

Through Him who made reconciliation the final word over *us*, may we likewise seek the good of our neighbor (1 Thess. 5:15) until our supplication bursts forth, "'May peace be within you.' For the sake of the house of the LORD our God, I will seek your good" (Ps. 122:8–9).

Midair

Joseph's brothers were highly informed. Despite the passage of years and the seemingly victorious concealment of their shrewd plot, their consciences had not effectively dulled to the calamity they had caused their father's favored offspring. If anything, compunction prevailed with ardor.

As their long-estranged sibling charged them with being spies, remorse drenched their discussion among one another:

> Then they said to one another, "Truly we are guilty concerning our brother, because we saw the distress of his soul when he pleaded with us, yet we would not listen; therefore this distress has come upon us." Reuben answered them, saying, "Did I not tell you, 'Do not sin against the boy'; and you would not listen? Now comes the reckoning for his blood." (Gen. 42:21–22)

Regret also enveloped their hopeless defense to their accuser:

> So Judah said, "What can we say to my lord? What can we speak? And how can we justify ourselves? God has found out the

iniquity of your servants; behold, we are my lord's slaves, both we and the one in whose possession the cup has been found." (Gen. 44:16)

A saturated lament coated their reply. In no way were they audacious enough to claim blamelessness when the lifeblood of the innocent was on their hands (Jer. 2:34–35).

Yet Joseph was the interesting one. For each of his reactions parses how a forgiving person operates; or rather, he clarifies—through his challenges to his brothers, through his crumpling in tears out of their sight—how trust and forgiveness do not function on a shared plane. For he exemplifies the willfulness to receive back to himself the ones who had wanted him dead—a feat that, through God's mercy, can be achieved void of the offending party's experiencing regret. But he also demonstrates how severe exploitation and misconduct cannot be overlooked with a nonchalant, automatic acceptance.

Pardon can toil, and even flourish, within a vacuum. The object of forgiveness, in even his most belligerent stance, can hinder nothing of the flow. A soul truly determined to bless another functions independently, with no contingency plan if the efforts are completely spit upon (see Rom. 12:14, 17–21), for the work is rendered freely by the one "doing the will of God from the heart" (Eph. 6:6).

Trust, in contrast, will never be unilateral in substance. When it comes to restoring confidence in the steadfastness of a person's character, especially if the last point of contact brought treachery or deception which obliterated any vestiges of integrity, offering unbridled fellowship would be as productive as constructing roofline trusses midair, with no framing supports beneath. Rebuilding necessitates interdependence: a willingness on behalf of both the offender and the offended to make efforts in a united direction.

For the one who has committed the wrong, proving one's mettle becomes a necessity—not for the sake of safety necessarily but for proof to the eyes of *both* parties that there is a wholly new starting ground, that the rubble of the past will not portend future interactions.

Joseph has been criticized by some as lording it over his brothers, challenging them unfairly with the hard tasks of bringing his full brother Benjamin to him (Gen. 42:20), binding Simeon before their eyes (v. 24), mysteriously restoring his brothers' money to their sacks (v. 27) and tucking his silver cup into Benjamin's sack (44:2) right after his unnerving the brothers by seating each at the table in their birth order (43:33). The fact that Joseph refused to speak with his family members without an interpreter between them (42:23) could be construed as a "mind game" as well.

But think what Joseph needed to hear! This man—who had spent years managing the household of an officer (39:1) and the prisoners beside his own cell (v. 22) as well as an entire nation's food supply (41:46–49), all since his harrowing venture in a Midianite caravan (37:28)—did not need to hear a mournful apology, especially if his brothers' words were "smoother than butter" but their "heart was war" (Ps. 55:21). Severed from every member of his kin for more than a decade, and emotionally overwhelmed when these men returned to his presence (see Gen. 42:24; 43:30; 45:2), his pierced spirit demanded the reassurance of true contrition, as he overheard his brothers' fretting over the indelible mark left by their long-standing transgression against him. There was solace in their ready acknowledgment and acceptance of blame.

He needed as well to meditate upon the fulfillment of dreams, in light of these siblings who had touted they would never bow before him (Gen. 37:8)—though the Lord had other plans (Gen. 43:26, 28; 44:14). To observe with his own eyes that "every word of God is tested" (Prov. 30:15) was to taste resplendent relief: that God, the Skillful Avenger, who "exacted full vengeance for him" (Jer. 51:36), had "vigorously pled his case" and brought him rest (Jer. 50:34). He witnessed firsthand the eviscerating truth that "the exercise of justice is joy for the righteous, but is terror to the workers of iniquity" (Prov. 21:15).

Added to his beholding man's confession and God's culmination of His sworn oath, Joseph required the convincing of a changed heart. As Judah concerned himself more with the sacrificial protection of one of their brothers than with his forfeiture of his personal liberty (Gen. 44:32); as he willed to forestall any further harm to his aggrieved father or the youngest son whom Jacob loved (44:20), the burgeoning testimony peaked: this man—standing before his Hebrew-speaking, Egyptian brother—had grown to disdain the man he had been, or else he would not have fought so adamantly to distance himself from past tactics. His practice of sacrificing others to preserve self had, through a set of humbling circumstances (Gen. 38:26), been upended.

The tests Joseph chose were not unreasonable. Faithfulness demands a proving. What is remarkable is not that Joseph engineered such a heavy hitting examination, but that his underlying intent shines through: that he refused to curtail the hope of reconciliation if there were any evidence of transformation. With humility and love, he was willing to receive to himself those who had egregiously wronged him, not because his empty-handed, famished brothers had anything to present him. He extended his heart toward them—he made himself known to them (Gen. 45:1) and drew them close (v. 4, 10, 14–15) and vowed to provide for them (v. 11) because of the testimony he could furnish them about the Lord, his God.

As he ministered to his relatives, he faithfully supplied each of these ten men the consolation that God's plans had been fully advancing amidst their treachery! He declared to them the holy purpose at work, as the Lord preserved life and wrought great deliverance (Gen. 45:5, 7, 8) on behalf of many (Gen. 50:20).

And, on an even more intimate level, God ministered to *Joseph*. By setting into order all the pivotal events that would place Joseph's brothers on his royal doorstep during the heart of the famine, the Lord pronounced His utter mindfulness over a betrayal that could not have been thoroughly resolved apart from the brothers' re-entry into his sphere. God was declaring in no uncertain tones that even the most prestigious circumstances in which Joseph found himself (Gen. 41:40–44) could not, in their exaltation, eradicate the hideous anguish of being personally shunned by his kinsmen (see v. 51). Arranging for the brothers to be directly involved in Joseph's mending, He gave them passage into Joseph's former wound and allowed them to discover that he bore them no ill will.

And in that providential renewal of contact, as these reunited brothers experienced each other's presence again, God conducted a caliber of healing in which the accrued damages no longer composed the concluding statement. Instead, by His sovereign favor, all the discordancy met its beautiful resolve in the vivid demonstration that love blesses in the highest degree, and longs for the preservation of life (Ezek. 16:6)—even and especially the salvation of those who incited the rupture to start.

Dedicated to M. E.

Never before had I heard a child shriek as she did. With my attention elsewhere as the class filed into line, I was preoccupied as this young girl's friend tumbled down the tar-blasted ramp. Following the shock, the boy's howl of pain left an even more damaged-looking visage on the face of his companion, who—with instinct only—wailed over his soreness, "Oh, I wish *I* was Edward!"

What eight-year-old thinks that way? Or, in my treating her demeanor as a rarity, does the incredulity betray my self-preservation? Am I loath to admit that, while an unbelieving child could immediately react to a dear friend's pain in a more Christ-like way than the teacher who asserts she belongs to Him, I am completely void of any such gut response? Do I hate that it never would have occurred to me to insert myself in another's trauma if it meant his sparing?

Shame should wash me brightly, for there is no bridging those mindsets. Nothing but mutual exclusivity presides—and I know on which side a believer should fall. Yet why am I found so backwards?

Have I succumbed to the deception that self-care is of topmost priority, that people are too messy and my own sores are demanding enough? Have I fallen for the lie that only Jesus had the task of taking on another's burden—emptying

Himself, bearing our curse—but (since no one else can be the Savior) we will never have to step into another's life-and-death agony? Have I set myself up as "exempt," with hands too lazy to work, a heart too reticent to bleed, and a spirit too wont to discount the adversity endured by those around me?

It would be one thing to peruse the Scriptures and find His unique claims—that He is the only Savior (Hos. 13:4), that there is none like Him (Ps. 86:8)—and surmise that our hands are not responsible for the dirty work of any kind of substitutionary exchange. That conclusion would be in error.

For, while it is altogether true that we are not qualified on any basis to redeem another, as we cannot even save ourselves (Rom. 5:6), it is equally true that the Holy Spirit has been sent to inhabit us for purposes redemptive in value—and those, not solely for our sake. In other words, for as hard as the admission is, the reason I have not been removed from this life yet is because my un-deadness now preaches to those who are still perishing (2 Cor. 2:15).

As one who is called to salvation that I "may gain the glory of our Lord Jesus Christ" (2 Thess. 2:13–14), and who has "become an heir of the righteousness which is according to faith" (Heb. 11:7), have I anything to lose? Were I to truly gaze at the distinctions, what could my hands so tightly grip in this life that would outweigh what a dying man in need of rescue could experience? Would throwing myself into the ordeal of unfounded hatred, unjust oppression, or unnerving disparagement prove a loss if accomplished "for the sake of those who are chosen, so that they also may obtain the salvation which is in Christ Jesus and with it eternal glory" (2 Tim. 2:10)? I doubt Stephen would think so (Acts 7:59–60).

And, interestingly, from the mouth of one who was

rescued from darkness and transferred to the kingdom of the Beloved (Col. 1:13), we learn of precisely what that intentionality entails. As the man at whose feet were laid the robes of those stoning the first martyr (Acts 7:58), the Apostle Paul, corrected in his vision of Christ as Lord and longed-for Messiah (Acts 9:1–5, 18–20), labored with every fiber of his spirit to testify to both Jews and Greeks of "repentance toward God and faith in our Lord Jesus Christ" (Acts 20:21). In addressing the believers who had come to him from Ephesus, he explained, "But I do not count my life of any account as dear to myself, so that I may finish my course and the ministry which I received from the Lord Jesus, to testify solemnly of the gospel of the grace of God" (v. 24).

The crux of his statement indicated that any fruitful ministry—of testifying to the grace of God through the gospel—would be hindered explicitly if he held onto his life as "dear to himself." He could not expect a completed ministry, a fulfillment of the course delineated for him by his Saving Lord, if he comported himself as one who loved his life in this world (John 12:25). Fruitful harvests only come through death (v. 24).

While our reflection of Him is sketchy and inconsistent at best, we are of those who delight to do His will (Ps. 40:8). In His mysterious act of grace, where we come to cherish His gifting of Himself to us, we are becoming vessels who are recognizing that our hearts were not reconciled to the Father's for the sake of indulging our selfish desires (1 Pet. 2:16), but that, newly freed, we could finally express His love through service (Gal. 5:13). As those who no longer crumple under the indictment brought against us by the accuser (Rev. 12:10), but who have ourselves been "plucked from the fire" (Zech. 3:2), may we revel to discern that those who are made overcomers now have the fullest leeway to nct love our life even when faced with death (Rev. 12:11)!

An Empty-Handed Guest

Time is unforgiving. When we are undergoing a troubling experience, its passage seems to slacken as a foot-dragging sort of protest. When we have emerged from the rubble, its irretrievability seems the taunting mess of what we'd ought not venture to recover. A substance most fickle and untrustworthy, it is nothing we dare set our hearts upon.

For a child whose parental neglect has left no happy childhood "tucked into one's pocket," for a teen who has plowed into a haze of narcotics that leave reality distant, for an adult whose efforts to live at peace with an irreconcilable spouse have availed more estrangement, and for those followers of Christ who have been rent asunder from family members because a godless government thought to hand down a prison sentence, there forms a tear-stained amalgamation of irreversible hours. Specifically, for those who are processing the peculiar fallout of actions that wrought wasted days there is the vivified discouragement: misspent hours are void of recourse.

To consciously rescind the pursuit of what can never be recuperated is a full-time labor in itself—because we are forced to focus on yet one more dimension of the powerlessness during that predicament's interval, but also because it seems a salty punctuation mark to an event that already upended our innards. Were it as simple as being able to draw from another source the reserves we would have kept at our disposal, then we would contend with no rearview mirror. Yet it is because of our temporal existence, accentuated by what time has un-gained for us, that we are blatantly left with the fact that we are heading toward a limit (James 4:14).

And yet, strangely, in that truth lies hope! For the God, in whose hand are our times (Ps. 31:15), calculated flawlessly our "appointed times and the boundaries of our habitation" (Acts 17:26). When Jesus told His listeners that they were incapable of adding a single hour to their lives (Matt. 6:27), it was in recognition that our Maker has written all the days that are ordained for us (Ps. 139:16). As Moses taught the Israelites to pray in Psalm 90, "teach us to number our days, that we may present to You a heart of wisdom" (v. 12), God-fearing acceptance of all He has allotted causes us to bow rightly and live circumspectly.

Yes, this is the God who formed seasons for our welfare (Gen. 1:14); who acted to both stop (Jos. 10:13) and reverse (Isa. 38:8) time when confirming His work on behalf of His people; but this is also the One most pointedly cognizant that "we are but dust" (Ps. 103:14). He has made no selection to our detriment.

But how do we process that another person's havoc has left us crumpled with "debts"; that time has demanded a hefty payment and we have been obliged to satisfy it? Job 34:13–15 gives us some direction as we linger over where to point our thoughts, for the question essentially asks, "Is not even our very breath from Him?" And if that ownership strikes us uncomfortably, may we be reminded that the Sovereign who chooses how our days are apportioned is the same who instills in us prayers for His recovery, not for a backward angle on what has transpired but for an about-face that puts our history in perspective.

For God's economy is different. With His beloved servant Moses, the most humble man on the earth (Nu. 12:3), God set a limit that Moses many times spoke about with His Maker (see Deut. 3:26). And while the Lord honored His word to show Moses the Promised Land from a distance, his days expired sooner than Israel's entry. Yet God's denial in the temporal realm actually ushered him into the "perfect" for which every soul longs.

Perhaps it is because we disproportionately value what can be found in this home that isn't really (Heb. 11:14–16) that we still mourn so intensely what we desire to be restored. Perhaps because we cannot even envision what awaits those who have placed their trust in Him (1 Cor. 2:9), we lack the affinity for what is to come. Yet the One who is leading us has withheld nothing from His children that will not ultimately prove to our undiminished benefit.

For even Moses, when contemplating the days his people had seen evil, was prompted by the Lord to ask that He "make them glad according to the days He had afflicted them" (Ps. 90:15). So the prophet Jeremiah also reported to the exiles that God had not forsaken His own with calamity, but was still pressing on to provide the nation with "a future" (Jer. 29:11). And Joel likewise elucidates how all that had been stripped would somehow be years the Lord would "make up" (Joel 2:25). We have no notion of what that repair work may entail, but we know the Giver of the promise.

And so, graced with that divine *coda*, we look not to things as they are outwardly, which are wasting away

(2 Cor. 4:16), but at the eternally satisfying truth: that the mission of our hours here is not with the aim of ultimate disgrace but with the *captivation* of unbelievers and the *conforming* of those already "captured" by His love. In light of the "forever pain" (2 Thess. 1:9) we rightly deserved for our defection from the purely Blameless One, all the resources we most prized here in this short span shed their illusory meaning. For in "insult, distress, and persecution ... for Christ's sake" (2 Cor. 12:10), and even in the seeming wastefulness of hours not to be recovered, we discover the inherent worth of "slipping" from our hands that which is lesser.

To welcome the empty-handed guest—that trial which strips us entirely of all we thought worth preserving—we are likewise stripped of seeking our own interests in lieu of Christ's (Phil. 2:21). Divergent are the paths that cling fiercely to irrevocable trinkets in this life and that flame with hunger for our first Love (Rev. 2:4).

By imitating our Loving Conqueror (Eph. 5:1–2), who endows each foe vanquished by grace with His own heavenly spoils[68] (see Eph. 1:3–8), we resonate with His manner of depletion. We are not receptacles to be indulged or repositories to be imbued with all assortment of earthly comfort but conveyors to a sin-sick world that "Hope has given Himself to the worst."[69]

And as we tread the footsteps of Him who invited to Himself an earthly existence depriving Him of the heaven He left, we are free to issue forth, with hearty approval, that all our days are deposited into the tender keeping of Him "who loves us and released us from our sins by His blood" (Rev. 1:5).

"Let Me Hate"

No commission of the Lord is born of injustice (see Ps. 5:4; 92:15). He has told us what is good: "to do justice, to love kindness, and to walk humbly with our God" (Mic. 6:8). We stand in no violation of the law (Gal. 5:23) to conduct ourselves on such terms.

More comforting still, He requires nothing He has not first fulfilled on our behalf (Matt. 5:17; Rom. 10:4), and He enables all who are His to follow by His Holy Spirit's equipping (John 16:13; Acts 1:8). A fluid response on our part is birthed in the overflow of abiding in Him (John 15:4–5).

Yet we may find in ourselves the musing that not every difficulty has been useful or necessary. The tearful writhing may seem the most "gritty" selection the Father could have meted out. It is then, especially on those "long-term assignments," that we must take at face value how He has been both purposeful and merciful in all He has appointed (Ps. 119:67, 71, 75; Lam. 3:33).

Rather than calculating the difficulties of what pardoning another entails or gazing bleary eyed at the pricey-ness and suggesting more palatable alternatives, we can advance into the joy of giving—less so for the one causing our injury and more so for the One to whom we have caused immeasurable injustice. What liberating hymns are lifted when we cry to our Beloved Redeemer, "You hated my sin for what it did to me; let me hate my sin for what it did to *You*."

Yet stumbling blocks inevitably come. Particularly when we are resolved "to be pleasing to Him" (2 Cor. 5:9), out of reverent gratitude for the Man upon whom our sins were laid, the internal fight against His command arises. Though His nature, as the Author of those precepts that bring our advantage, underscores our reasonable compliance, our selfish ambition (James 3:16) exacerbates every vile element within us that pegs His method of forfeiture (Rom. 15:3; Eph. 5:2) as unsustainable and unjustifiable.

The Apostle Paul, whose experience of hardships fills nearly an entire column of 2 Corinthians 11 (v. 23–30), asked the pointed question in a prior letter to this same flock. "Why not," he adjures, "rather be wronged? Why not rather be defrauded?" (1 Cor. 6:7). Why not prefer to submerge all of our alleged liberties and license into the One who commissioned us as ambassadors of another kingdom (John 18:36–37)? God will see justice through (Isa. 30:18; 61:8; cf Ps. 94:1), but foolishness alone impels the nursing of grudges (Eph. 4:26) and the desperate cleaving to vanities in this fleeting life (Heb. 11:25–26).

It quite pleases the devil when we vie adamantly for supposed "portions" that can be enjoyed nowhere but here. In zeroing in on peripherals, our self-lauding, self-exalting flesh languishes for every "right" to be observed. We revert to the "boastful pride" that is not from the Father but from the world (1 John 2:16).

And we also place ourselves at odds with the One who faithfully employs brokenness. If our Redeemer had set the pattern of "self-defense," perhaps we could be justified, but He left us void of any such argument. If anything, we can—through His humility and then exaltation—only attest to the truth that has been noted, "It is doubtful God can bless someone greatly till He hurts them deeply."[70]

And yet, when we are prone to losing sight of why God has sanctioned us to be on the receiving end of hostility, it may behoove us to glance again at some of the reasons (a smattering among countless scores) whereby His choice for the sake of others and ourselves was satisfactory and superior.

In certain cases, the Lord may be endowing us with His yearning nature (see Matt. 23:37) to bleed for the brokenness of the unbeliever, long for the wayward home, and surrender any personal gain for the restless soul to be set free. With the somber pleading unmarred by any of the hurting this world can inflict, we may be torn into the labors of beseeching that the Lord would remove the veil as a person turns to Him (2 Cor. 3:16). The alignment of our wills with His desire (1 Tim. 2:4; 2 Pet. 3:9) may dominate our every petition. The purpose may be to form in the wells of our soul a *compassionate conviction*.

There may also be an evangelistic endeavor marked out by the invasive nature as we make His presence known. When our lives compose the platform upon which the wreaking of travesties occurs, we become the eventual reminder—a sort of tassel that keeps the onlooker cognizant of his transgression (see Nu. 15:38–39)—of the pivotal factor in his repentance. The eventual shame that the Lord can bring to bear upon a life that receives new eyes may provoke this changed being to proclaim his abominations (Ezek. 12:16) in light of God's unfailing mercy. The purpose may be to foster a God-honoring, *penitent preaching* in a newly birthed soul.

At still other times, we may simply be sharpened to detect how selfishly and shortsightedly we bore into our own paths and pleasures, all at the cost to the Man who had committed no sin or injustice (1 Pet. 2:22). Our eyes might gradually awaken to the hardened audacity, the tenacious vice-grip, the quickened self-reliance, and the taunting insolence that have defined our stride and reckoned us unfit for God's use or indwelling in our natural (hell-bound) state. We may finally come to terms with the reality that we have nothing to offer and nothing to repay this Heavenly Being, who—of His own volition—irrevocably bequeathed to the disobedient His unsearchable and unfathomable gift of mercy (Rom. 11:29–33) where justice was deserved. The purpose may rearrange us with a *reverent recounting* of His marvelous dealings.

As we quit our resentment of the structure overlaying these lives, and freely resolve to grow into the maturity of Christ our head, we come to respond aright to the gift He has imparted: that the joy of giving after His fashion is indeed where the blessing lies (Acts 20:35)!

> He has honored us with His death;
> let us honor Him with our lives!

Afterword

While nothing can be added to the Gospel, it is the pulsing beat of the believer's life that bears repeating on a host of levels for the sake of grounding us in "the wonders of redeeming love and our unworthiness."[71] The news of heaven-sent reconciliation can never be sufficiently explored. Perhaps that is why believers are gifted with all of eternity to discover and adore the myriad facets of Christ's excellence, with every angle gleaming His brilliance.

May our hearts, patterned for His sake to forgive others, revel frequently and unashamedly in God Himself restoring to relationship those who would have otherwise been irretrievably estranged from Him—the only One good (Ps. 119:68; Matt. 19:17).

Reconciled!

God, who is morally spotless and completely blameless (Ps. 5:4), chose in His graciousness and mercy (Ps. 86:15) to reveal His nature to a creation He desired to make (Col. 1:16; Rev. 4:11)—not because He was in need of anything (Acts 17:25), but because He willed to show Himself as the covenant-keeping God (Deut. 7:8–9) who reconciles and restores (Luke 15:21–24; Philem. 1:17–18).

The only constraint God laid down was that His creatures revere His authority by obeying one command: to eat freely of any tree in the Garden, except from the tree of the knowledge of good and evil (Gen. 2:17). Within that command He also gave the promise that death would be the result of failing to heed His words (see also Ezek. 18:4, 23, 32). When His own creatures, made in His image, acted treasonously against Him by devoting themselves to their iniquity rather than to His rule (Rom. 1:21–23), His words were proven true, both in the spiritual and physical death that ensued. Adam, and by extension all of humanity, rebelled against God's rule, so that we no longer had any means to please Him or enjoy communion with Him. By that one act of disobedience, we alienated ourselves from the life He gives (see Eph. 2:12) because of our hostility against the Holy Creator (Col. 1:21).

But God, being an abundant Provider (Gen. 22:8; Lev. 17:11), had planned before the foundation of the world (Rev.13:8) to be the Mediator Himself (1 Tim. 2:5)! Treating the traitorous ones as "objects of compassion" (Ps. 106:46), He gave His own lifeblood as our Substitute. Making Himself of no account (Phil. 2:6–7), He condescended to our blood-guilty souls, and repaid God the two things we were beholden to present Him: either the righteous living that heeded His command, or the rightful dying for our clear-cut failure (Rom. 5:18–19). Christ was crucified in the place of those who had, on every level, affronted the Father and degraded themselves—by taking the form of a man (yet, even so, without shedding his Deity). After leading a morally flawless life, in which He continually honored God by loving Him with all His heart, mind, soul, and submissive will, He then stepped into our death sentence by being the One who gave to God on our behalf the poured out blood (Matt. 26:28; Heb. 9:22) necessary to satisfying the Law under which we had condemned ourselves (Rom. 3:19; James 2:10).

And the glorious news is that God didn't remain dead (Matt. 28:6)! Instead, "Christ 'died' death!"[72] Although He was in the grave for three days, just as He had foretold multiple times (Matt. 12:40; 16:21; 20:18–19), yet even the beaten and slaughtered Savior could not remain dead, because it was impossible for Him to be held by death's power (Acts 2:24). He returned to life on the third day, to those eyewitnesses who had walked closely with Him during His earthly ministry, and to hundreds of others (1 Cor. 15:5–8). His Resurrection not only declares Him to be the Son of the Living God (Rom. 1:4), but also demonstrates that there is no further need for God to remain hostile toward us

(Ps. 7:11; Rom. 5:9), since that which was offered to Him covered in full our once outstanding debt.

Christ, having conquered death (Heb. 2:14–15) and torn us from our slavery to sin (Rom. 6:17–18), was given all authority (Matt. 28:18) as reward for His faithful labors (Phil. 2:8–11)—for the sake of obeying His Father and for the sake of bringing near, through His own sufficient blood (Eph. 2:13), those who had rendered themselves defectors from the Immortal and Perfect King.

He has also given us His Holy Spirit (Eph. 1:13–14), having "cleansed our hearts by faith" (Acts 15:9) and given us adoption in His Son (Rom. 8:15–16). He has completely exonerated us before God (2 Cor. 5:21). We will one day be presented before Him as holy and blameless (Col. 1:22; Jude 1:24), but until that hour—while we still struggle against our disobedient and self-glorifying tendencies—we cling to the precious promise that it was "the Father's good pleasure ... to reconcile all things to Himself" through Christ, "having made peace through the blood of His cross" (Col. 1:19).

Praise the One whose righteous right hand accomplished salvation (Isa. 63:5), and has left us as recipients of His merciful declaration: *"No longer condemned"* (Rom. 8:1)!

Endnotes

1 ABC Curriculum (Units 1–10), *Answers in Genesis*, 110.
2 Paul Washer, "God Crushed Jesus Christ to Save Wretched Sinners," August 22, 2011, HeartCry Missionary Society, video, 4:30, https://www.youtube.com/watch?v=vvkqmUygsCU.
3 Noah Webster 1828 Dictionary ("forgive") 1828.mshaffer.com (accessed October, 2014).
4 Matthew Henry Complete Bible Commentary on 2 Corinthians 5:16-21, BibleStudyTools.com (accessed January 16, 2010).
5 Modified version; submitted to GBF Press (February 2017).
6 Milton Vincent, *A Gospel Primer for Christians: Learning to See the Glories of God's Love* (Focus Publishing, 2008), 12, 15.
7 Bryan Lee, "Christ and Cancer: My Only Hope in Life and Death" from *Grace Notes* (GBF Press, 2015), 10–11.
8 Bible Study Fellowship, Romans 5:1–11, Lesson no. 8, Notes, p. 6 (November 10, 2017).
9 David Crowder* Band, "Oh, Great God, Give Us Rest," *Give Us Rest or (A Requiem Mass in C (The Happiest of All Keys))*, 2012.
10 Dietrich Bonhoeffer, Berlin (1933).
11 Ibid.
12 Horatio G. Spafford, "It Is Well With My Soul" (1873).
13 Switchfoot, "I Turn Everything Over," New Way to be Human (March 23, 1999).
14 Pedja Ilic, "Armenian Genocide: The Battle of History, Justice, and Geopolitics," *San Jose State University*, January 26, 2015, 19.
15 Brian Fisher, "Because We Were Rescued," *Human Coalition* (formerly Online for Life), HumanCoalition.org (accessed March 30, 2018).

16 Marshall Segal, "When Our Hearts Revert to Self-Reliance," DesiringGod.org (June 30, 2016).
17 Ibid.
18 James Bynum, Evangelist.
19 Adam Clarke commentary on Deuteronomy 15, StudyLight.org (accessed December 9, 2012).
20 Matthew Henry Complete Bible Commentary on Deuteronomy 15, BibleStudyTools.com (accessed December 9, 2012).
21 Ibid.
22 2 Corinthians 4:17 (Phillips).
23 Thomas Kelly, "Stricken, Smitten, and Afflicted" (1850).
24 Charles Wesley and Thomas Campbell, "And Can It Be that I Should Gain?" (1738).
25 Dr. Cliff McManis, on Acts 9:1–5, Grace Bible Fellowship of Silicon Valley.
26 Kathy Yarrington, Bible Study Fellowship discussion, Romans 7:1–25 (December 6, 2017).
27 John Newton, "Amazing Grace" (1779).
28 The Rev. Charles H. Spurgeon, "David's Dying Song, Sermon no. 19 (2 Samuel 23:5)," April 15, 1855, Jesus.org.uk (accessed July 13, 2018).
29 Carla Bergen, Romans 12:9–21, Bible Study Fellowship lecture (March 14, 2018).
30 Blog published February 18, 2008; modified April 5, 2018.
31 James Bynum, Evangelist.
32 Dr. Craig Milco, Acts 9:10–19b; Luke 6:32–35, "When Our Souls Can Breathe Again," quoting Emma Timmons, *Lark Rise to Candleford* (season 3, episode 2), BBC (November 10, 2013).
33 Bible Study Fellowship, Romans 11:33–36, Lesson no. 20, Notes, p. 1 (February 28, 2018).
34 Matthew Henry Complete Bible Commentary on Matthew 5, BibleStudyTools.com (accessed July 27, 2018).
35 With some insertions from blog published September 3, 2006.
36 Oswald Chambers.
37 Dr. Derek Brown, Sunday School series on Luke 4, Grace Bible Fellowship of Silicon Valley (September 13, 2015; September 20, 2015; September 27, 2015).
38 The Rev. Jonathan Edwards.

39 Bernard of Clairvaux (translated by Paul Gerhardt, James W. Alexander); Johann Walther, Hans L. Hassler, J. S. Bach, "O Sacred Head, Now Wounded" (1153).
40 The Rev. Charles H. Spurgeon, Sermon no. 320 (Philippians 4:11), March 25, 1860, 93 Best Spurgeon Quotes, Pinterest.com (accessed May 3, 2018).
41 Joseph Bayly.
42 Andrée Seu Peterson, "Faith Is the Thing: Believing in the Absence of Receiving," *World Magazine* (February 21, 2015).
43 Joni Eareckson Tada, *Revive Our Hearts* calendar.
44 C.J. Mahaney, Jude 1b, "Called, Beloved, and Kept," *Resolved Conference* (2011).
45 Bernard of Clairvaux (translated by Paul Gerhardt, James W. Alexander); Johann Walther, Hans L. Hassler, J. S. Bach, "O Sacred Head, Now Wounded" (1153).
46 Blog published June 19, 2007; modified July 18, 2018.
47 Stuart Townend, "How Deep the Father's Love for Us," *Thankyou Music*, 1995.
48 Carol Wolfe, Guest Speaker for Grace Bible Fellowship's Ladies Retreat (April 1, 2017).
49 Dr. Derek Brown, Luke 8:1-15, "The Parable of the Soils," Grace Bible Fellowship of Silicon Valley (June 26, 2016)
50 Matthew Bridges, "Crown Him with Many Crowns" (1852).
51 Gregory Koukl and Tim Barnett, "Hell Interrupted, Part 2" from "Solid Ground: A Foundation for Building Ambassadors," *Stand to Reason* (November/December 2017): 3.
52 Switchfoot, "The Economy of Mercy," *Learning to Breathe* (September 26, 2000).
53 Bishop of Smyrna (A.D. 69–156), ChristianHistoryInstitute.org (accessed March 20, 2018).
54 Pastor Matt Chandler, "God Is for God," Code Orange Revival (January, 2012).
55 Blog published December 5, 2009; modified March 22, 2018.
56 Katie Barcay Wilkinson, "May the Mind of Christ My Savior" (before 1913).
57 Messianic Jewish song, *Congregation Harei Yeshua*, Paradise, CA.
58 Brigit Hull, Bible Study Fellowship discussion; Book of Romans (November 29, 2017).

59 Modified excerpt from message "Forgiving One Another," delivered at Grace Bible Fellowship of Silicon Valley (October 25, 2014).
60 Noah Webster 1828 Dictionary ("pardon") 1828.mshaffer.com (accessed October, 2014).
61 Ibid.
62 Dr. Cliff McManis, "After the Resurrection," Grace Bible Fellowship of Silicon Valley (April 27, 2014).
63 Kathy Wolff, Bible Study Fellowship lecture (December 14, 2015).
64 Bible Study Fellowship, Romans 1:18–32, Lesson no. 2, Notes (September 28, 2017), 5.
65 Dr. John Piper, John 19:30.
66 Noah Webster 1828 Dictionary ("reconciliation"), 1828.mshaffer.com (accessed April 11, 2018).
67 The Rev. Jonathan Edwards, "The Resolutions of Jonathan Edwards," DesiringGod.org, posted December 30, 2006 (accessed July 24, 2018).
68 Carla Bergen, Romans 11:1–32, Bible Study Fellowship lecture (February 14, 2018).
69 Switchfoot, "Living Is Simple," *Learning to Breathe* (September 26, 2000).
70 A. W. Tozer, quoted by J. R. Cuevas, 2 Corinthians 12:7–10, "Dealing with the Thorn in the Flesh," Grace Bible Fellowship of Silicon Valley (August 21, 2016).
71 Elizabeth C. Clephane, "Beneath the Cross of Jesus" (1868).
72 Dr. Cliff McManis, Grace Bible Fellowship of Silicon Valley.